LIVE FROM
THE KENAI RIVER

Reeling 'em in
with Alaska's Celebrity
Fishing Guide

**Harry Gaines and
Lewis Freedman**

Stackpole Books

Copyright © 1991 by Stackpole Books

Published by
STACKPOLE BOOKS
Cameron and Kelker Streets
P.O. Box 1831
Harrisburg, PA 17105

Printed in the United States of America

First Edition

10 9 8 7 6 5 4 3 2 1

Library of Congress Cataloging-in-Publication Data

Gaines, Harry.
    Live from the Kenai River : reeling 'em in with Alaska's celebrity
fishing guide / Harry Gaines and Lewis Freedman. — 1st ed.
      p.   cm.
    ISBN 0-8117-3029-8 : $14.95 ($19.95 Can.)
    1. Chinook salmon fishing—Alaska—Kenai River. 2. Gaines, Harry.
3. Fishing guides—Alaska—Biography. I. Freedman, Lewis.
II. Title.
SH686.2.G35 1991
799.1'755—dc20   91-9757
                                            CIP

Contents

Introduction

You'd think that by now Harry Gaines would have paid me off to shut me up. Instead, I'm writing his life story. I guess he really does have a sense of humor.

You see, by all rights I should be his greatest embarrassment. It's his job to help people catch fish in the Kenai River in Alaska. I tried four times to catch a king salmon with Harry Gaines and I got shut out. Four times. Every time. And not only that, I tell the world about it every time in the *Anchorage Daily News,* the local news-paper.

I should explain. I never went fishing in my life until I was well into my thirties. I grew up playing basketball, baseball, a little football, and running cross-country and track-and-field in a suburb of Boston. I had no acquaintance with the outdoors. My view of the outdoors was that it was the usually humid, or often freezing, place that you had to walk through to go between two buildings. Nature? Well, I had heard of the birds and the bees. That was about it.

Go fishing? Not even to meet girls. Let's play ball. That was my philosophy.

I never even had the urge to go fishing until I'd lived in Alaska for a couple of years. It took me that long to overcome my deprived city upbringing.

Once upon a time, when I still thought a king was the leader of a country, silver was change you received for a dollar, and a red was a person of the Communist persuasion, my relationship with fish consisted of staring at them from the other side of a glass bowl.

Several years of living in Alaska, however, changed my outlook.

All my friends, neighbors, and coworkers would chant, "Gotta get a king! Gotta get a king!" each spring. They were not talking about getting King Juan Carlos of Spain to attend one of their dinner parties. No, they were talking about king salmon.

I was curious as to what could transform otherwise rational humans into salivating fools, what could persuade mostly intelligent folk to sit outside in pouring rain for hours doing what looked like absolutely nothing.

I was loath to relinquish my claim as the Only Man in Alaska Who Does Not Fish, but upon investigation, I concluded that there was much more to this fishing thing than the average transplant from a major eastern city might have thought.

If you are going to go fishing, you must find out where the fish hang out. So you drive down the highway to the Kenai Peninsula until the Winnebagos are thicker than the mosquitoes. Then you're there.

Actually, you must also get a fishing license. During the summer, Alaska Department of Fish and Game agents go by their 00 prefixes and are licensed to kill. For ten dollars you get permission to pretend to catch fish for a whole year.

And if you wish to be more scientific about finding places where red, silver, and especially king salmon hang out, then you hire a scientist. That's how I first came to meet Harry Gaines during the summer of 1987. He was my scientist.

For my first fishing trip, I was placed in a boat with Gaines and two of his grandsons, Sam, then fifteen, and Pat, then twelve. I was willing to bet they both knew more about fishing than I knew about all other sports combined after a lifetime of watching "Wide World of Sports."

Harry baited the hooks for all of us, using little red salmon eggs, then delivered a pep talk. Most of his clients are first-time king salmon fishermen, he said.

"Yesterday, I had a seventy-five-year-old guy who never fished a day before in his life, and he caught a fifty-three-pounder," said Gaines.

The message was clear. Anybody, even I, could catch a king salmon, with no previous experience. And clearly, the fish were everywhere. I was about to say something about this when I felt a jerk on the end of the pole.

Gaines winked. "That's my trained fish," he said.

We drifted with the current and periodically pulled our lines in and rebaited the hooks when the eggs had gone pinkish from too much time in the water. Gaines would rev up the outboard motor to move us to another spot on the river.

Gaines's boat was outfitted with all kinds of neat state-of-the-art stuff. It had a little plaque on one end reading, "Early to Bed, Early to Rise, Fish Like Hell, and Make up Lies." And it had a hand-held depth estimator.

This was all entertaining, but after hours of sitting on the Kenai, I was beginning to understand why all those restaurants found it easier to come up with filet mignon than king salmon steak. Sam had briefly hooked and lost a king. I had hooked the middle finger of my right hand. It didn't bleed much.

While we were out, Harry did his regular live fishing reports for a local radio station. On one of them he said the fishing was probably a three on a scale of ten. For me it was a zero.

Once in a while Gaines would try to appeal directly to the fish. I thought his folksy, down-home Texas accent might fool the fish into doing something rash.

"Here fishy, fishy," he said. "Talk to the fish," he urged me.

I knew deep down that the fish would detect the hint of a Boston accent in any words I uttered, tagging me as an imposter fisherman.

"There's a fish out there with your initials," said Gaines.

Not that day, though.

One year after relinquishing my title as the Only Man in Alaska Who Doesn't Fish, I tried again. This time I knew I had to buy a fishing license before I could try to fish. I even knew that I'd better wear a hat, a sweatshirt, a light parka, and boots to stay warm. That's what you call experience.

The fish were not impressed.

I came to realize that seduction was all-important. In my mind Southern speech loomed more and more important as a technique. A random sampling of conversations with friends seemed to support this theory. Those who spoke slowly and sounded as if they were born near the Alamo or in Scarlett O'Hara's backyard were more likely to have king salmon parts inhabiting their freezers.

I resolved to learn how to talk.

Time passed. No nibbles. No chomps.

"Just start talking a little bit slower," Gaines advised.

No nibbles. No chomps.

My analysis of the situation grew more sophisticated. The problem, I theorized, was that the fish and I kept different hours. Yeah, that was it. The fish preferred swimming their laps at dawn. I preferred sleeping till noon. So by midafternoon, when I was out on the river, they were taking naps.

More time passed. Still no nibbles. Still no chomps.

My pole jerked. Gaines saw the movement out of the corner of his eye.

"Was that a hit?" he asked hopefully.

Regrettably, I had to inform him I was just shifting my arm so that it wouldn't cramp.

"You did that on purpose," he said.

No nibbles. No chomps.

"Are you always this lucky?" Gaines asked.

For my third king salmon fishing trip, Harry convinced me that I absolutely had to go fishing in the early morning. This is a heretical suggestion to someone who works nights and who doesn't believe in breakfast before noon (and then only when it's called lunch).

I did it anyway. I went fishing at five-thirty in the morning. Five-thirty? There is only one place to be at that time of day, and it isn't in a fishing boat on the Kenai River.

After coming no closer than rumor to any king for two years, I was scaling down my goals. All I wanted to do was *see* one. I didn't have to hook one, never mind catch one. Just see one to prove Kenai kings aren't a mirage.

One flaw with this approach was readily apparent: at five-thirty in the morning, when stuff was being loaded into the boat for our six o'clock pushoff, I couldn't see a thing. My eyes were closed.

So that the day wouldn't be a total loss on the boat — Gaines knew me too well by then — he also booked a young honeymoon couple, Kristen and Dennis McEvoy of Westford, Massachusetts.

After less than an hour on the river, Dennis had hooked a fish. Quickly reeling in, Kristen and I tangled our lines spectacularly. It was Keystone Kops fishing. Gaines looked on in horror. Dennis lost the fish.

The fish must have come up while I was goofing around with the line, taken one look at who was in the boat with Dennis, and in a desperate attempt to save its self-esteem, escaped.

Just to make Dennis feel good, Gaines said, "That was probably a new world record." I think he was trying to sow the seeds of dissension in the boat.

"C'mon Kristen, a little lady luck this morning," said Gaines.

We motored up and down the river on a very pleasant day. All around us people weren't catching fish. I must have jinxed the whole Kenai River.

Dennis remained confident. About four hours into our six-hour journey, he proclaimed that he would catch his fish about eleven-thirty, just before we packed up.

"When are you going to catch yours, Lew?" Harry asked.

"About 1995," I said.

As the morning ticked away, Gaines stared at me. "You're due," he said.

Overdue.

A few months later I received a package in the mail from the honeymoon couple, who didn't seem to hold a grudge against me for scaring away all the fish on their one-and-only fishing trip in Alaska.

Inside the wrapping was a fancy box printed with the words "Collectors Crystal Galleries by Fairfield." This is nice, I thought as I pried open the top.

Inside the box was a tin can of pink salmon.

When the summer of 1990 rolled around, I considered waving a white flag. The king salmon were leading on the scoreboard three to nothing, and I hadn't even sniffed the end zone.

I didn't expect the results to be any different for my fourth attempt at catching a king salmon. That day it was incredibly tranquil on the Kenai River. It was so quiet and there was so little competition for fish that I found myself compelled to thank Harry for clearing the river for me to improve my fish-catching chances.

I felt a tug at the end of the line. Could this be? Did I really have a fish on?

I reeled in quickly, and there she was, a true beauty, the prettiest stick I'd ever seen. It was slender, about two feet long, and with nice bark. It was a heck of a catch, if I do say so myself.

After that trip I went home and reported abysmal failure once again. I was hoping for sympathy. Instead, I ended up with my own kid making fun of my fishing prowess. On Father's Day yet. Sigh.

So after four years I have not even come close to hooking a king salmon. Reports of my failures continue to appear in the pages of the *Anchorage Daily News,* and fishermen all over the state continue to get a chuckle at my expense.

I deserve it. Anyone who goes fishing with Harry Gaines time after time and doesn't catch a fish is obviously a guy who is all thumbs, who doesn't have the brains to walk and chew gum at the same time, or who should take up shuffleboard as his next new sport.

But Harry hasn't given up on me, so I won't give up on him. I'm going to catch a king salmon with him one of these days. Make that one of these years.

—Lewis Freedman
September 1990

First Fish

It has been said that the truth will set you free, and even if no one believes an old fisherman when he starts spinning yarns, I figure I'd better be truthful from the start.

Otherwise my wife will tattle on me.

The truth is, the first fish caught in Alaska by the Harry Gaines family was not caught by Harry Gaines. Actually, the first salmon we caught in Alaska was lost by Harry Gaines. It was not a good start for a fella who would eventually come to make his living as a fishing guide. Catching the fish and keeping them is the idea most of the time.

It was the summer of 1970, and my wife, Dot—short for Dorothy—and I drove out to Bird Creek, which is about twenty-five miles south of Anchorage. It's a beautiful creek right off the highway, with rushing water that feeds from Cook Inlet.

Lord, the fish would come in there. They were red salmon. During the high tide they would enter the creek in large numbers. The water was usually so clear you could see them through the surface, and they would be moving fast. On this day, though, the water was very dirty. You could see the fish some of the time, but other times you couldn't see a thing.

We were standing on the bank and I cast and I cast and I cast. Nothing doing. Then Dot hooked a red, a nice one, six or seven pounds. She hooked it and was playing the fish. The fish fought back and started jumping around. She finally landed the fish and used the tip of her rod to hold the fish to the ground.

I put my rod down on the ground and went over to try to help her. Which seemed like a good idea at the time. Dot swung her rod around toward me, and I reached out, held the rod, and tried to grab the fish with my hands to land it. So I get my hands around this fish, around its girth, which is absolutely the wrong thing to do. I just didn't know that then. He wiggles and squirms and before you know it, he's in the water and gone. Oops. We stared at the water for a while as if he was going to come back and we'd get another chance at him. You know the feeling?

It got awfully quiet out there for a minute, and then Dot had a few words for me to let me know just whose fault it was that fish got away.

A man has to think fast in a situation like that. Catch and release, I told her. We believe in catch and release. She was ready to catch and release me but good.

You've got to start someplace in the guiding business, and I learned some lessons from that experience. For starters, you don't grab a fish around the middle like that with your bare hands. You grab the fish by the gill plate, or you go into the mouth, though some fish have teeth to watch out for, or even grab them by the tail. If that fish moves too much, it will break its back. Better than that, you should use a net.

But I guess the biggest lesson I learned is that you don't take someone else's rod and bring in their fish. Especially your wife's fish. There was no reason why Dot couldn't have landed that fish herself if I'd stayed away and minded my own business. Even now, twenty years later, and after taking thousands of people fishing, I will not take anyone's rod. If they have a fish, if they catch a fish, they're going to bring that fish in. I'm going to give them instructions, but I am not touching their rod. Unless they are having a heart attack. Then I might have to help out, and you know, that has happened.

Dot still blames me for losing that fish for her. It could have been my fault. Or maybe she just didn't have it hooked too well. Of course, that's not a possibility we've discussed at length over the past twenty years.

You'd have to say I'm a slow learner, though. Later that summer we went fishing at a lake and I helped Dot release a trout, too. Heh, heh. It was probably a world-record lake trout. Take it from me, all fish that get away are extremely large. It's the best way to remember them.

Now that I think about it, my son Jimmy Don caught a salmon in Alaska before I did, too. We were living in Anchorage, in an apartment downtown on Third Avenue, and we frequently went over to Ship Creek. That's just a few blocks away and you can fish for kings there sometimes. They have a dam built there, and some people go over there just to watch the fish jump around in the water and swim up and over the dam. Sometimes they jump nine or ten feet. It's quite a sight. There's probably no other large city in the world where a person can see king salmon rushing past like that only a few blocks from the heart of a downtown area.

One day, soon after we moved to Alaska, my daughter Rebecca and my two sons, Jimmy Don and John Harry III, went down there. A little later, Jimmy Don, who was about sixteen years old at the time, comes running back to the apartment yelling, "Look what I got! Look what I got!" And he had himself a king salmon that weighed twenty-five or thirty pounds. It was just cradled there in his arms like a baby. He actually caught it by hand.

I think the boys got in the water and pushed the salmon out and caught it with their bare hands. But the problem was, it was illegal. It was out of season. What was I supposed to do with it? Of course, it was too late to take it back: it was dead. We cooked that fish up and had it for dinner.

So my wife had hooked a salmon, and my son had caught one, and I hadn't. A few weeks later, though, we took a family fishing trip to the Kenai River for the first time and we caught pink salmon. We limited out. I think the limit was three per person at that time. Even I caught them. We had so many fish we brought them back to Anchorage, ate them, put some in the freezer, and canned some more.

That was probably the first time I realized just how special the fishing could be in Alaska. And I hadn't even hooked a king salmon yet.

The Mighty King Salmon

The king salmon is a special fish. It is a fighting fish, and the biggest kings in the world migrate to Alaskan waters. And that means that fishermen come from all over the United States and the world to try to catch one.

That's the main reason I've been a successful fishing guide for over twenty years. They want the experience of catching big fish and I take them to big fish. The average sportsman in the United States just doesn't have the opportunity to catch big fish. They dream of catching the world record. And they can do it. It's a real challenge to catch a king salmon and to feel the strength of that fish pull on the line, and it's a thrill to see it lying there in the boat afterward.

The fish is pulling. The current is pulling at about six miles an hour. There's excitement. The fisherman knows the biggest fish he's ever caught is on the end of the line. I'm shouting encouragement. When the fisherman finally nets that fish, he's just thrilled.

The king salmon is one of the largest sport fish a person can catch, but one of the other attractions is that fishing for kings doesn't require going out into the ocean. There's accessibility. It doesn't hurt any that we're in Alaska, a place with great allure and mystique, and it doesn't hurt any that the Kenai River is not only one of the most beautiful rivers in a beautiful setting but is also easy to get to. It's easy to get to the Kenai Peninsula. You can fly on a commuter plane from Anchorage every half hour, or you can drive a few hours, and the river is right along the highway.

Beautiful area or not, though, people come for the salmon, king salmon foremost among them. Even a king that weighs just twenty-five pounds is so much larger than other fish anyone will catch in lakes or rivers in the Lower Forty-Eight states that they're all prizes.

Most American fishermen, and most from around the world, will never see a fish that weighs more than a few pounds. They fish for trout or perch or catfish, whatever the local specialty is. Those fish might weigh three pounds. So to them the king salmon is a monster. They come hungry to catch one, bring it home, and brag about it, and you can't blame them at all.

The world-record king salmon caught in sport fishing on the Kenai River weighed 97¼ pounds. Les Anderson, a local fisherman from Soldotna, Alaska, the town next to Kenai, caught that fish in May 1985.

Do you know how big a fish like that really is? Why, it's the size of a child going into the fifth grade. A king like that, or even a sixty-pound king, might be four feet long. That's a fish to remember.

When a client gets a big fish on, I tell everyone else in the boat to reel in their lines, sit down, and be quiet. They've got to leave that person alone and let him bring in his fish.

I coach them. "You got it!" I tell them. "Reel! Reel! Reel! He's running." I talk them through it. I talk them into bringing the fish into the boat. It's their fish and later they're going to want to say that they caught it. And they did!

I've actually had people down on their knees in the boat, begging me to take the rod and help them. And I'm telling them, "You can do it. You can do it." And they do it.

That's what they pay me for and it's my philosophy to let them bring the fish in. Most of the time it's psychological and I can convince them and they do it.

I'm sure that's the right way to do it, but as always, there are exceptions to the rule, and one of those exceptions scared me to death.

In the mid-1980s, a man from the Midwest was on the boat and he hooked a king salmon. I was there, as usual, telling him he could do it. I wouldn't take the rod, even though he asked me to. Sweat was breaking out on his forehead. He fought the fish a long time. Then he said he felt funny and he fell to the floor of the boat. He was gripping the rod so tight I couldn't get his fingers off it anyway.

He was a man in his sixties, and after he brought the fish in he was just exhausted. He was just limp in the chair. It wasn't until afterward that his son told me he'd had a heart attack and triple-bypass surgery about a month or so before. I began to shake a little. It made me real nervous. I'd been hard on this guy, too. He was asking me for help and I wouldn't give it. I felt terrible. If I'd known the circumstances, I would have helped the guy.

Finally, after a while he began to relax and we got him back to the shore and called for an ambulance.

But you know, he did catch the fish. He got his fish.

That will show you how desirable king salmon are. This man almost died for one.

As I said, the king salmon is a special fish, but other kinds of salmon also spawn in the Kenai River. You've got kings, you've got red sockeye, you've got silver salmon, and you've got the pink salmon. In different parts of the country they're known by different names. The pink is also known as the humpy. The silver is also known as the coho. The red salmon is also known as the sockeye, and in some places the king is also known as the chinook.

Let's stick with the king for now. In late April, the king salmon begin to enter Cook Inlet on their migratory path to the Kenai River. They start entering the Kenai in very late April or early May.

The Kenai River is my home. It's where I work, and in the summers it's also where I live, about fifty feet from the water. There aren't many rivers in the rest of the United States that have the same kind of beauty as rivers in Alaska.

On sunny days, when the sun glistens off the water, you're looking at turquoise green water seemingly inviting enough to drink from. It's a spellbinding color, and the question I am most often asked when we're out fishing is what gives the river its color. It's glacial melt. When the snow melts in the spring, the water runs off into the river, bringing with it silt that is several million years old from the glacier.

The Kenai River is eighty miles long. It runs from Cook Inlet all the way over toward Seward. But when you're talking about where I fish the Kenai River, you're referring to the first twenty miles of river away from the mouth. That's the stretch where the action is.

There's a glacier that feeds into Snow River near Seward. Snow River feeds into Kenai Lake. Kenai Lake feeds into the Kenai River, which feeds into Skilak Lake, which feeds back into the Kenai River and comes right down to Cook Inlet.

For one period in the middle 1970s, there was a lot of heavy fishing done in the midsection of the river, and that would be from the town of Sterling, which is about twenty miles north of Soldotna, to the Soldotna Bridge.

The fish move through the lower river very fast. They are fresh and lively. At one time they would congregate in the midsection of the river. But for some reason the fish changed their pattern.

No one knows where the salmon go when they go to sea. The fish that return to spawn are generally three to five years old. It's unknown why they return to the same places or how they do it. The first run of kings occurs at the very beginning of May. Actually there are some kings in the river by April 27 or 28 each year.

It's as if God made a calendar for the fish and the fish follow that calendar. It's just nature. It just happens every year. The way we used to test to see if the first kings were in was by fishing from the bank. It's always that time of year, within seventy-two hours. We don't really start fishing heavily for kings until a little later, though—about May 15, when you know there will be many more kings. But I've caught a king as early as May 2.

Then there's a second run in late June, and they run all the way through July. The first run of salmon, meanwhile, goes off to some of the tributaries of the Kenai and spawns.

Anywhere up to six or seven weeks after they've entered the Kenai River, they have spawned. They lay their eggs mainly on gravel bars. The female will take her tail and shape a trough and lay her eggs. The male will come along and fertilize the eggs. Each male takes care of four to six females and then covers up the eggs in the gravel. That's the male's job.

After that the salmon don't eat anymore. Once a fish begins the spawning process, it never eats again, and it's pretty hard to interest one in biting at bait on a hook. Those fish, you'd pretty much have to put the hook in front of their nose to make them snap at it. After they've gotten that far into the spawning process, they're starting to die. They will strike, but really they're starting to deteriorate. They deteriorate from the outside in. Their organs are still functioning inside. They start to turn red in color. Most kings headed upriver to spawn are in their prime and still have a silvery appearance, though some older ones do take on a red cast. I don't know if that's from abuse or what, over time.

The salmon live off only their own body fat from the time they hit fresh water. In fact, their throats begin to close up as they follow the migratory path up from Cook Inlet. They just shut off eating altogether, as if they've forgotten how to do it. Occasionally, I'll open one up and find something in the stomach, but very seldom. Usually, it's a dry stomach. There's nothing in the intestinal tract at all. After they lay the eggs, they go off to die.

The eggs don't hatch out until the next spring. They go through the winter months buried in the gravel. The next spring they hatch and you can watch them in the river as they begin to migrate to the sea. It takes them a year to do that. They stay in the river, in fresh water, for a year. Some of them are only as long as your finger when they decide to go to sea, and when they do, you don't see them again for three years or more.

There really hasn't been any scientific research to find out where they go. Maybe there's a fear that if we followed them and found out where they were going and monitored them, foreign fishing fleets would take advantage of them.

It's my feeling that, because they're a bottom fish and because some of their diet is shrimp, they just stay on the bottom of the ocean somewhere. Another thing that tells me that might be right is that not many are caught except when they're migrating. The fishing fleets are out there with tremendous nets and they catch huge amounts of fish. But the only time you hear about them taking in king salmon is during the migration period. I may be off base, but that's my personal belief.

Another thing no one really knows is why some fish stay away longer than others. But they do come in schools of various sizes. It's a common belief that the biggest kings in the Kenai come in the second run.

Scientists have a way of checking ages by scale samples. Occasionally when you're fishing, a biologist will pull up next to your boat and ask if he can take a scale sample. So he takes a sample from a fish, records where the fish was taken and the date it was caught. Under a microscope that scale has rings just like a tree has. That's how the Department of Fish and Game knows whether the fish is three years old or nine.

The longer a fish is out in the ocean, the more it weighs when it returns. The older fish are the biggest ones. I'd guess that a fish averages ten pounds of weight gain a year because the four- and five-year-old fish are anywhere from forty to fifty-five pounds. The six- and seven-year-old fish are sixty, seventy, and seventy-five pounds.

The world record would be an old-timer. I would guess the world record would be maybe ten or eleven years old.

It's my theory, actually, that there's a third salmon run, of large fish only, that is much smaller than the other two runs and mingles with the second run. The Alaska Department of Fish and Game will not agree with that. But the larger fish are a slightly different color, almost brownish, and you've got to remember that the average fish in the first run are thirty-five to forty pounds, and they say the average size of the second run is fifty to sixty pounds.

Yet the world record was taken in May. And in that same year we caught an untold number of seventy- and eighty-pound fish around the first of June.

I think there's a group of fish that hang out together for years, for whatever reason. The research is lacking. It's going to take years to get several generations of the fish to study. In the meantime, I've got a theory and someone else has a theory. But over a period of time I've seen those huge fish congregating.

You know, the fact that the world record was taken in mid-May makes you wonder. What if the biggest kings of all are the ones that are coming in singly in April? Maybe we're missing the biggest ones altogether. Just a thought.

Early Days

I am not one of those people who always knew exactly what he'd turn out to be in life. Not at all.

I may be a fishing guide now, but it was many years before I came close to realizing that fishing in Alaska was the profession for me. In fact, I was almost forty years old before I came to Alaska.

Like so many Alaskans, I'm not originally from Alaska. I was born in Waco, the heart of Texas, on August 16, 1930, during the Depression. So I was a Depression baby.

I grew up in Waco and went to Waco public schools. Waco is the home of Baylor University, but it only had 40,000 or 45,000 people in those days. I'd bet they have almost that many students at Baylor now. Paul Quinn College, a predominantly black school, is there, too. I went to Baylor but really spent less than a year there.

My dad, Harry Sr., was a fireman and a police officer. He was born in East Texas, lived in Fort Worth until he married my mother, Evelyn Fenton, in 1929, and then moved to Waco. My dad's family, though, was originally from Georgia. Fort Gaines and Gainesville, Georgia, were named for his ancestors. There was a General Gaines in the Civil War from my family, too. My mom's family was from Missouri. Her dad and mom once had a farm next to Jesse James and the Dalton Gang.

We had a really good family life. It was me, my dad, my mom, and my sister Sarah Evelyn, who is three years younger than me. There was a twenty-year age difference between my dad and my mom. Dad was thirty-nine when they got married and Mom was nineteen, but something that I remember from growing up that was really, really important to me was that I don't recall them ever having an argument. Never in my life.

It was a good family life, but I was itching to get out on my own. The times were different then—World War II was going on—and kids didn't seem to stay at home until after high school and then go right on to college. I didn't. I felt I was mature and wanted to start my life, and my parents didn't hold me back. I didn't have problems at home or anything, but by the time I was fourteen or fifteen years old, I had a small apartment. I went to high school while I was living away from home, and I worked evenings in a bakery. My parents didn't fight me. They wanted me to get an education, but they helped me when I was living in the apartment.

Growing up back then was so different. Educational values were more important than they are today, but learning was different. Your ability to learn seemed more important. You didn't have all the computers and fancy calculators. You had to learn for yourself. You had to rely on yourself.

After a while I wanted something better than the bakery, and I applied for a job as a magazine salesman. I got the job, and I went off selling magazines like *Redbook, Liberty,* and *The Saturday Evening Post*. The job required that you be eighteen years old, and I wasn't, but I faked it, and they believed me. I wasn't particularly big, so maybe I was born just looking old. Or maybe someone just wanted to think I was of age, because they sent me to Houston and San Antonio, and for four to six weeks I made pretty good money. I don't remember how the company found it out, but the next thing that happened was that someone did realize I was underage, and they paid my bus fare back to Waco.

I did stay with school, but also I was always working. One summer I sold mops door to door. Fifty cents an hour was considered good pay. Fifty cents or seventy-five cents an hour was enough for me to get by on.

Some of the time I was back home, some of the time I was on my own, but I did eventually graduate from Waco High School and start college at Baylor. I kind of came and went there, too, though.

One of the things I remember about my childhood is that my mom and dad were great fishermen. Maybe I inherited the interest right there. At least they were an influence. They loved to go fishing. Every free minute they could get, they would go fishing. We were

This is me at age eight with my dad, Harry Sr., and "a mess of fish."
The year is 1938.

out fishing once or twice a week year-round. They loved it. It was an early introduction to the sport as a fun thing to do. My father and some other firemen shared a fishing camp. It was shared property and each family got a little piece of acreage. You could build a little cabin on your piece. We had a trailer. The communal area had a dock and a hundred-foot-long pier.

The earliest recollection I have of a family fishing trip — my first-ever fishing trip — was in 1936. I was six years old, and one of the reasons I remember it so clearly was that it was a cold, wintry, blustery day. It was real cold. We went out fishing in our newly purchased 1935 Ford. You'll see in a minute why I remember that car so well.

We went to Lake Waco. Lake Waco was an open lake. By that I mean there weren't trees right up on the shore. There were just a few wooded areas, and you could see some mountains in the distance. We fished for perch, white perch. They weighed about one to three pounds. They were babies compared with a king salmon. We would use cane poles with cotton fishing line, and on the end was a bobber or a cork. Minnows were bait.

On the day of this particular fishing trip, as I said, it was very cold, and my sister and I got quite uncomfortable. We must have done some complaining because my parents put us in the car and left us there while they went back to fishing on the lake.

Naturally, as soon as I got warmed up, I got bored and started looking around for something to play with. Well, there was a butcher knife laying there in the car, and as we all know, boys will be boys, right? I picked up the knife and started slicing up the seat. I cut the ribbing of the seat right off. This is our brand-new car.

And there was a cigarette lighter in this brand-new car, so I tried the cigarette lighter out. You know how kids will get fascinated with things that are bright and beautiful, and that cigarette lighter fit the description, all right. So I branded my sister Sarah on the leg with it.

That was my first fishing trip. I did catch some sun perch, about three or four inches long. They're flat, multicolored fish, little things. They were the first fish I ever caught. But I also caught hell on my first fishing trip when Mom and Dad got back to the car. Let us say that they did not spare the rod when they got a good look at the car and got all the details from my sister.

Lake Waco was pretty close by and it was a productive lake, so we didn't go far to fish. No big, extended trips. Once we went to watch the building of Lake Texoma, on the Texas-Oklahoma border, and we watched them drive those bulldozers to build dikes and expand the lake.

But it was mostly fishing in Lake Waco. It was easy just to shoot on up to Lake Waco. About the biggest fish we ever caught were catfish. They weighed about four or five pounds. That's typical of fishing in most of the Lower Forty-Eight states. The big fish are just small fry by Alaska standards.

We caught fish, but we didn't catch fish in great numbers. We called it a mess of fish. It was enough for eating for a family dinner. Or we'd have a fish fry and invite all the neighbors over on a Sunday afternoon.

At that young age, from the time I was six to about fourteen, I don't really have much recollection about liking fishing or disliking fishing as something to do itself, but I enjoyed going to the lake and fishing with my family. It certainly never crossed my mind at that point that I would ever fish for a living. Who even knew such a thing was possible?

One thing that I learned as a kid fishing with my parents was that you never give up. Because regardless of how cold it was, we'd go out and fight those fish. I remember going out in extremely cold weather. Of course, extremely cold weather by Texas standards was quite different from extreme cold in Alaska. If it was forty degrees, we'd consider that real cold. Up here in Alaska, that's summertime.

After my dad retired, he and my mom did begin to expand their fishing territory. They went all over the country fishing. That's what I plan to do, too, when I retire — fish all over. I'll be following in their footsteps, just fifty years later.

Once I started working, the fishing trips with my family came to an end, and I didn't have much time to go fishing myself. You'd have to say that making a living cut into my fishing time. That was way before I discovered that a person could go fishing all the time and still make a living.

Fishin' and Talkin'

Pretty much most of my life, I've made a living either fishin' or talkin', as I like to say. For the last fifteen or twenty years, it's been fishing *and* talking. I've been a lucky guy to be able to do what I want.

I got my start in radio just about forty years ago, and I'm still on the air almost every day in Kenai. In the summer it's live fishing reports about ten times a day from the boat or the house, and in the winter I still do a regular talk show early in the morning. The radio is secondary to the fishing now, but that wasn't always the case.

Looking back, it seems obvious that I was destined to be a fishing guide because I love to fish and I love to meet new people and show people a good time. It just took a few years for all those things to mesh in my life.

I suppose that growing up in Texas I thought about being a cowboy, just like other kids. I was living in the Wild West, you know.

Really, though, I didn't know what I wanted to be. All kids want to be a policeman, a fireman, or a radio announcer. You go through stages in life. Whatever you want to do, you can do it. That's always been my philosophy. I've done a lot of things in my lifetime. Some of them were odd jobs, and some of them were just odd careers.

For a while I thought I had a future in music as a performer, but I did not have a voice. I found that out quickly enough. I just couldn't sing. I had Harry Gaines and the Heart of Texas Playboys, a country and western band, going for a while. If I could sing, I would be on top today. We used to play lots of shows around Waco and, in fact, played the music at my high school graduation dance.

I also had a pop band. This one was called Harry Gaines and the Dipsy Doodles. I didn't really play in the pop band. I booked them and I emceed, I introduced the songs. We wore real stiff clothing — black pants, white shirts, bow ties. It was a real spiffy little band. If the high school was doing a talent show or something like that, we'd be the backup band. If there was an opening of a store around town, we'd get a call and provide the entertainment. It was not to be confused with Carnegie Hall, I'll tell you that.

The country and western band all dressed alike, too. I remember one time going to a J. C. Penney fire sale to buy all-red shirts. This was a real fire sale. The shirts were on sale because they'd been water damaged. My mother embroidered the name of the band on the backs, and that was our uniform. That was a big thing to a high schooler.

We played nightclubs, and we had a regular booking at the Odd-fellows Club. Every Saturday night they had a dance and invited the public. Families would come. It was just a big open room, and no liquor was served, just soda pop and popcorn. We did that for a good year.

We also had a Saturday morning radio show. I got up at five o'clock in the morning to go to this radio show, on KWTX in Waco, that lasted thirty minutes, from six to six-thirty. Not quite the same thing as the Saturday morning cartoons kids watch. But come to think of it, maybe it wasn't all that different. My mother wrote our theme song: "Hear our song as we ride along, the Heart of Texas Playboys." I don't recall the rest. She just changed the words to another song and fit that to the tune.

Just after us, from six-thirty to seven, another band came on every week and, boy, did we do some scrambling in that station because it was only a one-studio radio station. They'd move in and we'd move out, or they'd move in behind us. There was only a one-minute break for station identification and then they were on. We had to be quiet for them, and they had to be quiet for us.

There was a young man in this band I went to school with, and he was really popular in school because of his guitar playing and his singing ability. It turned out those fans were right — because his name was Hank Thompson. He sang with the Brazos Valley Boys and had hits like "Whoa, Sailor" and "Humpty Dumpty Heart." He went to the top and recorded million-seller after million-seller.

I'm the one in the back row dancing with the bass fiddle. These are the Heart of Texas Playboys (and some girls, too), in Waco, Texas. (Photo courtesy of Sarah Bood)

I guess I knew I was never going to hit it big with the Heart of Texas Playboys because of what happened with Hank. After a little while of those morning sessions, Hank and his group got on another station in Waco and were on at noon. Better timing, huh? And I was still on at six to six-thirty. The next thing I knew, he had gone on to Dallas and was on one of the big stations up there. He just took off like a blaze roaring across the fields and quickly became renowned in country and western music. And I was still on KWTX from six to six-thirty in the morning, once a week.

Soon after I graduated from high school in 1948, I was going to Baylor, taking some courses like radio speech and psychology, which, for some reason, included hypnosis. You'd have to say that both of those subjects played a major role in my life later on, but the radio course had the most immediate impact.

I had been in the radio class less than two months when I became friendly with another young man, Bill Williams. He was taking the course, although he was in his thirties and owned a radio station in Hillsboro, Texas. I was only twenty, but he took a liking to me and told me he had some ideas about establishing a second radio station in Waco, a remote station, broadcasting into the city from Hillsboro. Hillsboro was thirty-two miles from Waco, and Waco already had a radio station, but he said he could get a remote studio set up and I could be his manager.

Well, because of the distance from Waco and the low wattage of his station, you could barely hear it in town. It wasn't that successful. He had some difficulties in meeting his financial obligations. So I came up with an idea to save the operation. I said, "Listen, here's what we'll do. We'll take the radio station out of this big, fancy building that we're paying fifty bucks a month rent for [today it would probably be $2,000 or $3,000 a month] and we'll put it in my parents' home."

This is the kind of thing you always hear about in those old Mickey Rooney movies, right? You know, "Okay, kids, let's put on a show," and then they tear up the house and the backyard and whatnot. But this was for real. It sounded like some kind of joke or harebrained plan, but he went for it.

At the time my parents were on vacation, so I didn't even ask them. I took everything out of a bedroom in the back of the house, and we moved the radio station in and began to broadcast. We'd broadcast four or five hours from Waco, and the rest of the day they'd broadcast from Hillsboro.

Well, my mom and dad returned from their vacation, pulled up to the house, and saw three or four cars in front. They wondered what was going on. They got kind of scared. Maybe they figured bad guys were inside, looting the place. So instead of coming into the house, they went over to the house of my sister Sarah and her husband, and asked, "What the hell is going on over at our house?"

Sarah told them, "Harry set up a radio station."

They were kind of disturbed about me taking all the furniture out, collapsing it down, and putting it in a shed outdoors, but the radio station remained. It lasted about four months, from late in 1948 into 1949. I was on the air two to four hours a day, playing country and western music. I put on the records and read the commercials live. I still have a lot of the old 78-rpm records in the basement of my home in Kenai.

After the radio station business, I became an usher in a theater for a while. A big show came to town about 1950. It was a midnight horror type of show, a stage production, and I got myself into it by doing a mechanical man act. I put on white makeup, wore a tuxedo, put on a high hat, and carried a sign on my back. You know, you just walk stiffly. You make your limbs seem stiff and awkward. Someone else had been doing it, but he went on a big drunk and got himself fired. I said, "I can do that." I would put on the outfit and walk up and down the street outside the Orpheum Theatre to get people to come to the show.

I worked with a guy named Art Darner. He was Boris Karloff's double when he played Frankenstein in the movies. The show was owned by Republic Motion Pictures. It was a spooky show where they turned the lights out, waved fluorescent flags, and told you there were spiders on the floor. There was a magic act that went along with it, and the Frankenstein monster would make his appearance. People would be screaming and hollering and carrying on in the audience. It might sound a little hokey now, but in that era the special effects of modern movies didn't begin to approach the level of sophistication they've reached now.

All's I know is it worked. The audience was scared. The people running the show liked what I did and asked me if I wanted to join up with their traveling troupe. This is like the old stories you hear about kids running away to join the circus. Of course, I decided to do it. We'd use trucks to transport the sets, and we'd spend two or three days at each theater. It was like the circus in that way, though we didn't have to set up the big top. During my nine months with the show, I traveled to forty-five of the forty-eight states. We missed Oregon, Montana, and Washington; of course, Alaska and Hawaii weren't states yet. I made it to all of those states later.

I did the mechanical man act on stage, and I did hypnosis as part of the magic show. It was some scene. Sometimes I'd draw people out of the audience one at a time, or I'd do mass hypnosis. I'd put fifteen or twenty people to sleep at one time. This is how I got them hypnotized. I'd put a bunch of people in chairs in a row, count to ten, and ask them to focus their eyes, close their lids, and concentrate on sleep, and then to listen to my voice and my voice only. "Everything else will go away," I told them. "You won't be able to hear anything except my voice, and when I finish counting to ten, you're going to be sound asleep." I just kept repeating myself. I told them the only time they were going to react was when I called them by name or touched them. The rest of the time, they were supposed to just sit there and relax. Then, one by one, I'd have them do various things. I'd tell one person there was a washbasin in front of him, and I'd like him to wash his face. He would take a handful of water out of the air and wash. I'd tell one person he was a singer, and he'd believe it and sing for us, even if he couldn't carry a tune.

I'd suggest they put their hands together and would be unable to pull them apart, and they'd all be there tugging and twisting, hands stuck together. Or I'd have them stand next to a wall and put their hands flat on the wall, then ask them if they could get their hands off the wall. The hypnosis made it seem as if their hands were glued to the wall. We'd do all sorts of things.

If a volunteer looked as though he was strong enough, I'd stretch him out between two chairs, with his head on one chair and his feet on another, and I would stand on his body. You can't lie to people under hypnotic suggestion, but I would tell him he was very strong and repeat it several times. It took a minute or two to convince him.

Now I'm not that big a guy. I'm only about five-foot-six, and in those days I weighed considerably less than the hundred and eighty or so pounds I weigh in my old age. I weighed around 130 or 140. Even if I did weigh just 130, you will have to admit that if a person weren't hypnotized, he would definitely take notice of a weight like that on his chest. I never had anyone collapse when I stood on them.

I'd also plant posthypnotic suggestions, so when I woke them up, I could still get them to do things later in the show by saying a specific key word. Their orders were to react to one command until they heard another key word. That's how I got them going, running around the building shouting "Fire!" when they had gone back to their seats. That was followed up with another key word and some people started shouting "Water!" I had people running all over the place shouting "Fire!" and "Water!" and "Help!" and everything else. I suppose that's one way you could legally yell "Fire!" in a crowded theater. After I brought them out of it for good, they'd go back to their seats and not remember anything they had done.

Nowadays when people hear about my background in hypnosis, they ask if I can hypnotize a fish into jumping into my boat, or if I can hypnotize a fish into taking someone's bait. I've never tried it. You know that fish have eyes on both sides of their head? It would be a challenge staring into their eyes. And I'm not sure that telling them that they're sleepy is the way to get through to them. There are some people who fish with me who don't have very good luck whom I'd like to hypnotize into believing they'd caught a fish.

Seriously, though, there are some ways that the principles of hypnosis apply to my role as a fishing guide when I'm out in a boat with clients. In the same manner that I used to convince those people stretched out between the two chairs that they were strong, I plant the suggestion right from the beginning that when we go out on the Kenai River, we're going to catch fish. They believe when they get into that boat that they're going to catch a fish. And later, too, when we're out fishing and someone hooks a big fish and starts to get overwhelmed by how tough it is to get it into the boat, I'm doing the same thing. When people start saying, "I don't think I can handle it," I tell them, "You can handle it." I tell them they're going to bring it in alone, they can bring it in, there's no problem. Reel, reel, reel, I say. I talk them right through it. I guess that's one form of hypnosis.

The show ended its run around the country in December 1950, and I went back to Waco. Shortly after that I joined the Air Force.

My Life in Show Business

I guess I've always had a talent for promoting myself. Part of it is just having fun, but part of it is giving the people what they want.

One of my trademarks is my beard. It's thick, long, and flowing. But I didn't grow it until much later in life. I got the idea that when people come up to Alaska to see you, they have this particular idea of what an Alaskan looks like. They think all Alaskans live in the wild, and they all have beards, since they don't have electricity to use an electric razor anyway. So I began to grow it. I've had it just about down to my waist, past my belly button, two or three times. I keep it shorter now, so that when I look straight down, tilting my head, I can see an inch of it from my chin. It grows fast, too. I'm bald on the top of my head—that's why most of my clients never see me without a Harry Gaines fishing cap. Hair won't grow up top, but, boy, does it grow on my face. In the winter it keeps me warm, and I can comb it out neatly. It's not always blowing around in the wind like it does on the boat when we're motoring up and down the Kenai. If I shaved my beard off now, nobody would recognize me. People know me by the beard.

Besides, what would Santa Claus be doing without a beard? I've played Santa Claus every Christmas since 1971 for the Chamber of Commerce down here on the Kenai Peninsula. People already think I look like Santa Claus; I might as well be him. And I have to admit that dressed up in that red suit I do look a lot like the guy everybody thinks of when they think of Santa Claus.

Hey, everyone knows that Santa Claus lives in Alaska, anyway, right? My return address is Alaska, and I just tell people that Santa's summer home is Kenai. In fact, just a year or so ago, a friend of mine, Ken Graham, a professional photographer, took a whole photo shoot of me as Santa in the summer. He had me working with the flowers, out in the boat, doing all sorts of things. Santa without reindeer or snow.

Dressing up as Santa Claus is just another form of show business, I think — not much difference. I got my start in show business with that radio station back in Waco and that traveling horror show. Even my service in the Air Force involved more show business than fighting.

I joined the Air Force in December 1950, as an entertainment specialist. My job was to provide entertainment for the troops. During the day I was out doing my basic training, but at night I put on shows at the service clubs. The enlisted men's club, the officers' club, all of them. I kept perfecting my ability to do hypnosis. There were lots of times I wished I could hypnotize a superior officer into changing his mind on one order or another, but I never tried it.

As an entertainment specialist, I did a lot of USO shows and a lot of tours of government bases around the country. I emceed a lot. And when I wasn't traveling or doing a show at my home base, I had a full-time on-air radio job. I did the sign-on and station identification and pushed a lot of buttons. Most of that time was at Pine Castle Air Force Base near Orlando. One time, I remember, Walt Disney came to the area, and it was in all the newspapers. He bought the land that is now Disney World, but they didn't build on it for many years.

George Lindsey was one of my closest friends at that time. We were in the same unit. Later, when he got out of the service, George appeared as Goober on "Gomer Pyle" and on "Mayberry RFD." For quite a while he's been a member of the cast of "Hee Haw." George and I both had aspirations. We wanted careers in entertainment, though I still didn't know exactly what I wanted to do. Radio, entertainment, some combination of that. For years, throughout most of the 1950s, I was involved in radio in one way or another, or in one part of the country or another, although mostly in Texas and Florida.

At one time I worked for some people who had a recording studio in Dallas, and we had a show called "The Big D Jamboree," which was a country and western show, similar to "The Grand Ole Opry." Instead of being based in Nashville, it originated in Texas. As an

Me as a member of the Texas National Guard. It's about 1948, and I'm seventeen or eighteen here. Definitely officer material.

offshoot of that, we had a road show that traveled around the state every week. They used local talent, and we'd come along and bring in a star. We were on the air live. I was emceeing, and I also did some of the booking and promoting. In Austin, we called it "The Capitol Jamboree." In San Antonio, it was "The Alamo Jamboree." In Waco, it was called "The Cotton Palace Jamboree." It took place different nights of the week in different parts of the state.

I was working with them when Ray Price was discovered and also Lefty Frizzel. Those guys all got their start in Dallas. At the same time, I was freelancing on the radio at KLIF in Dallas. I had a lot of energy in those days, but it was fun. I was busy all the time, and I was meeting interesting people. We all thought we were going places.

Some of the people around then were Gordon McClendon, Lindsey Nelson, and John Cameron Swayze. This was long before Lindsey Nelson became famous on the game-of-the-week football, or with the New York Mets, and long before Timex for John Cameron Swayze. Gordon McClendon, a sportscaster who was called the Old Scotsman, originated his own network. It was called LBS, the Liberty Broadcasting System, and it had more than four hundred stations, plus Armed Forces Radio. Those were still days of innocence in broadcasting, clearly nothing like what we have today with remote feeds and other sophisticated equipment.

We originated baseball games in the basement of KLIF radio. These were major league games from all over the country. Wrigley Field in Chicago, wherever. You've seen this in the movies — in fact, Ronald Reagan did it during his early days in radio. We used sound effects and ticker tape. The play would come in over the ticker, just a short description. It would read, "Stan Musial up to bat. He strikes out." We added all the color. I might say something like, "Musial steps into the batter's box. Last time up he singled to center. Sal Maglie goes into his windup, stretches, and there's the pitch. It's a fastball and it's a strike. Just caught the outside corner." Of course, I'd have no way of knowing that. I'd just try to make it sound good and believable and add some drama to the game without changing what actually happened.

Then there were the sound effects. It would be the crowd reaction. For a strikeout in the home park, it might be an "ooh" or an "ahh." If a player on the home team hit a triple, there would be cheers.

I was just helping out. Lindsey Nelson did the play-by-play with Gordon McClendon. I was the guy who said, "This is LBS, the

Liberty Broadcasting System. We pause now for station identification." That was my main job. But I was associating myself with John Cameron Swayze. I thought it couldn't hurt me, that it would help me get ahead.

Eventually, though, the Liberty Broadcasting System folded, even if Gordon McClendon's wife did have a lot of money. She'd gotten it in the oil business. At one time he owned ten or twelve radio stations, plus the radio network reaching around the world. He owned stations in Houston, Oklahoma City, New Orleans, Shreveport, San Antonio, all over. His wife got him into all these businesses, and it all went flat. He had the idea that he could make anything happen, but it all went down the tubes.

John Cameron Swayze left for the networks, and so did Lindsey Nelson. We were all learning then, but they had been around a few years longer than I had. They had developed their skills there, and they had proper schooling, too, which helped them get on with the networks. I never really got formal schooling after high school except for those few courses at Baylor. That was one of my real problems in radio. I just didn't have a complete, formal education.

Back then, I never really thought those guys would become as famous as they did, but back then you thought you were famous. When you're working for a radio network that stretches all over, or you're traveling and doing shows all over, you have the feeling of being famous. Being famous now means being on the cover of *People* magazine, or on late-night talk shows, but radio was still king in the late 1940s and early 1950s. Television hadn't quite made its true impact, and there was certainly nothing like cable TV. So being on the air, being known as a radio personality, was a way of being famous.

At first, after I got out of the service in 1953, I stayed at the radio station in Florida, but after three or four months I decided I wanted to go back to Texas. I had a burning desire to work for a country and western radio station in Taylor, near Austin, because it was the station I'd listened to when I was a kid. KTAE in Taylor, Texas. It doesn't sound like very much, but it had a great deal of influence in country and western music.

This station had a live band called Jimmy Heap and the Melody Masters. They were on Capitol Records, and they were on the radio every day. Well, I ended up managing the band. They needed somebody to promote them, and that somebody became me. One of their recordings, "Release Me," was probably one of the all-time most popular records. They wrote it and were the first to release it, but Engelbert Humperdinck had a big hit with it much later, and sometimes I think half of America's recording artists jumped on that song, too. Jimmy Heap and the Melody Masters' version wasn't quite as famous, but they did get the royalties.

There were seven people in the band, and it played throughout Texas, but only places within driving distance from Taylor, because they had to be back to do the live radio show every day. Once in a while, if they were going to be gone overnight, we would record a thirty-minute show. That was a wild time, and it kept me on the go.

Jimmy drowned in an accident around 1980, but all the other members of the band are still alive. One day I was talking about them and I said to myself, "God, I wonder what they're doing?" I sat down and made some phone calls, and it was the first time I'd talked to them in twenty years. They were surprised to hear from me, especially from Alaska.

Another hot band I got affiliated with at that time was Sid King and the Five Strings. They were country/pop/rock. Music was changing then, just starting to move to rock and roll. I moved the band to Taylor and gave them a thirty-minute radio show, too.

There were five boys in the band and they all carried the last name King to make it appear they were all brothers. They weren't. One of their first recordings was a song that Carl Perkins had made, but they didn't do so well because Perkins's version was still popular. Later, another guy you might have heard of had a slightly bigger hit with it. The song was "Blue Suede Shoes." The other guy was Elvis Presley.

The band and I went a lot of places together. Now "The Grand Ole Opry" is famous all over the country, but then there were other regional shows that were hugely popular and had great followings. I took Sid King to "The Ozark Jubilee" in Springfield, Missouri, and "The Louisiana Hayride" out of Shreveport. Those guys were young, though, and kind of wild, and they became a headache for me, and we split up. They were partying too much, and I just didn't want any more of that type of thing. The group soon dissolved.

At one point in the 1950s I was a relief announcer on KWKH in Shreveport, following "The Louisiana Hayride." I'd fill in as the all-night disc jockey. I took off for Louisiana right after I finished my show in Taylor. I'd just drive like a bat out of hell from Texas to Louisiana. I was looking at six or eight hours of night driving. Airplanes were around then, but you just didn't fly for something like that. Entertainers traveled by bus. I did a lot of traveling by Greyhound when I was in the music business.

As I mentioned, KTAE had a major influence in country and western music. Taylor was a small town of maybe 12,000 people, but KTAE was the number-one radio station in Austin, even though it was forty miles outside of town.

One of the people just starting out with whom I came in contact was a young fellow we called Little Willie. He would come in for recordings with Ray Price, who sang "Don't Let the Stars Get in Your Eyes," but they wouldn't let this guy sing. They put him on bass fiddle, which was my instrument, too, when I dabbled in playing music. After a few public performances, when he did get to sing, he started getting more attention than Ray. When he sang, people screamed and carried on. This guy's name was Willie Nelson. He does have a voice.

During the time in Texas when I'd come home to the radio station of my dreams, I got involved in the gathering of news for the first time. I worked with a fellow name of Preston McGraw, who was the bureau chief for United Press before it became United Press International. In fact, it may have changed over during this period, 1953 or 1954. I started freelancing, feeding him stories, and I won a state award for generating the most stories as a freelance contributor to United Press for one of those years. I always did bring a lot of energy to whatever I was doing. I was writing the news and putting it on the wire. I'd cover things like visits from Lyndon Johnson. He was a senator then, still several years away from becoming president. I did talk with Lyndon Johnson on the telephone sometimes, but it was usually his press aides. I'd call over to his ranch if I heard something was happening, and I'd get a little interview. Then I'd call the UP office in Dallas and give them the story. The same way with anything that happened around Austin.

I became friendly with the Texas Highway Patrol. They'd come by and pick me up, and I'd ride around with them occasionally. That way I would pick up on things that were happening, like the crash of a small airplane. Then I'd run and call the bureau. They'd give me credit when it ran across the wires, "Harry Gaines, KTAE, Texas," and then dateline it Brant or wherever.

I covered a flood in Lampasas, which is fifty or sixty miles away from Austin, in the mountains. They wanted on-the-spot coverage and I got there an hour after it happened. Something like seventeen people drowned, a real tragedy. Because of my press affiliation, I was able to get in close to the bodies. Most were covered up, but they found one body still under a house. The house was built up on pilings, and some of the webbing washed away. The body just floated underneath it. I was tagging along with the rescue workers, and I still remember that body.

That was not the first time I'd seen a dead body, though. One of those odd jobs I had in high school was with an ambulance company. I worked at night and could sleep on the job unless we got a call. One time, we were called out at two o'clock in the morning, in a driving rain, for an auto accident. It was out of Waco toward MacGregor.

When we got there, we found two bodies lying on the pavement, covered up with some kind of cloth. The rear seat was taken out of one of the cars and made into a prop for the head of one of the guys. Their wives were there, and it was an overpowering scene. You could just look at them and tell they were definitely dead. We loaded them into the ambulance and took them straight to the morgue. I was about fifteen years old at the time.

I did many things from high school on, some for just a short period of time, some just to make a little money, some to try and get ahead. When you're young, you've got tons of get-up-and-go, and you never think you'll need sleep. Looking back now, I don't know how I squeezed everything in. A person can't live at that pace forever, but I was enjoying everything I was doing. I wanted to try this, and I wanted to try that. I was young and on the move.

On the move back to Florida, eventually. I contacted John Cameron Swayze in 1956, and he really helped me out. He pulled some strings to help me get a free-lance job with NBC radio, and I was assigned to Cape Canaveral. I lived in Orlando for two years and covered the development of the United States' outer space technology. This was the height of the Cold War and the time of Sputnik, when the Soviet Union became the first nation to launch a satellite, and America was rushing to catch up.

I guess the biggest job I ever did for NBC was on January 31, 1958, covering the launch of an unmanned satellite. That was the highlight of my news broadcasting career.

These days, whenever the United States launches a satellite or shuttle or rocket, we all know about it. They announce it and we all follow it. But at that time, they were still trying to keep things as secret as they possibly could. We did not have the liberty of going through the control room or even going on base. All the reporters who wanted to cover the launch of the satellite were put ten or twelve miles away, on what they called News Nob Hill. They just segregated us out there, and we observed the launching pad from a platform.

The only information they'd give us was that there was a possibility there would be a launch sometime in the next seventy-two hours. Be there, if you're interested. That didn't exactly narrow it down too much. So we'd go out there and wait. If you're not there, you don't get the story, and NBC is paying you for the story. I went through many times — three days and three nights — without sleep.

There were a lot of newspeople there. The government was trying to keep everything hush-hush, and we were trying to find out all we could. This was right after the McCarthy era, when Joe McCarthy had been getting public figures blacklisted, and people were scared. Anybody talking to a reporter was talking a little bit out of the side of his mouth, so that no one would accuse him of being a Communist.

There was an atmosphere of excitement surrounding the space program. There was a sense that something special was going on, and we were part of it, that we were watching history being made. We knew it was important because the Russians were ahead of us, but even more than that it seemed like fantasy was coming true, that Buck Rogers and the comic books were becoming reality.

The funny thing was, it didn't feel all that different from the time I was broadcasting on the radio station back at my parents' house. I didn't think, "Oh, God, there's a million, three million, five million people listening to me." It didn't feel big time, because it was a makeshift operation. We were out in the field, not in a big studio. It was exciting.

Just because I was in Florida, with news as my primary occupation, didn't mean I was away from country music altogether. It was in my blood. I loved it. I probably loved working in country and western music more than I loved fishing in those days, if you can believe that.

When I was working for NBC, I'd drive up to "The Grand Ole Opry" every week. It was during the old days, when they still had it at the Ryman Auditorium, and I'd be the NBC network announcer. I'd say the sponsor was RC Cola, Royal Crown Cola. It was a thirty-minute segment, and it featured Carl Smith and the Tune-smiths. I didn't have the world's biggest part. In fact, I still remember my lines. "WSM, the National Life and Occidental Insurance Company of North America, brings you "The Grand Ole Opry." RC! Royal Crown Cola! brings you the Carl Smith portion of "The Grand Ole Opry." Let her go!"

That was as close as I ever got to playing "The Grand Ole Opry." You know, that stretch of time in the mid-1950s was the only period in my life that I didn't fish. I spent all of my time trying to become a big fish, instead of trying to catch big fish.

The Legend of Another Big King

The big one that got away was not a fish. The big one that got away in my life was Elvis Presley. I'm probably the only person in the world who ever promoted Elvis Presley and lost money.

During the mid-1950s, when I was booking the singing groups and doing the radio show in Taylor, Texas, I came in contact with a man named Horace Logan. Horace was the producer of "The Louisiana Hayride," which was a country and western show originating in Shreveport, Louisiana, on Saturday nights.

Horace called me one day and said, "I've got a man I'd like you to book over in Austin."

Sure, I said. I'll try to do it.

He said, "Well, this guy is new, and he's only got a couple of recordings out, but we think he's going to be hot."

So I went after it. I called a friend of mine who owned a place called the Dessau Dance Hall, near Austin, and I told him I had this hot young property fresh off "The Louisiana Hayride," and he should draw well. It was a large dance hall that held two or three hundred people, and I thought it would be no problem getting a good crowd.

It was just an old Texas-type dance hall, a big building with a bar on one end and a dance floor with tables around the outer perimeter.

They agreed to give us $200 for the night. That was the contract agreement. Two hundred bucks for Elvis Presley.

Elvis came into town that afternoon while my show was on the air, and I met him. I interviewed him on the air. It was just a routine interview. I was building up the fact that he was playing the Dessau Dance Hall that night, and we talked about his latest recording.

41

He had a three- or four-piece band with him, and they came in a station wagon. He was wearing blue jeans and a white, western-type shirt. He was a very shy person, had little to say. It seemed at that time he didn't really believe he could sing, but he was doing well, off to a good start.

Back then I thought he was just another musician, just another singer. I was happy to meet him, though. I liked meeting any of the singers whose records I played.

Elvis Presley talked the way he sang, with that distinctive style. He was kind of an aw-shucks-type of fellow.

Well, Elvis Presley showed up in town and played the Dessau Dance Hall in 1955 or so. Whenever. And do you know how many people showed up? Nineteen. That was it. Nineteen people showed up to hear Elvis Presley. How many people do you think wish now they had been there? Or might say they were there?

Three months later Horace called up again, and they wanted to run him through the Austin area again. You would think I'd say, "No way," and point out that nobody went to see him the first time. But in between, just like that, Elvis Presley was starting to take off. I was playing him on the radio station, and I was getting more and more requests to play his music. I was getting fifty or a hundred cards a day requesting his songs. Elvis was really getting popular.

Elvis was just on the cusp then, and you've got to remember, so was the music. As I said, music was changing. We were going through a period when we had to ask, well, was it country and western? Was it pop? Was it rock? Was it black music? Sam Phillips, who owned Sun Records in Memphis, Tennessee, developed styles. He developed Elvis's style, Carl Perkins's style, Johnny Cash's style, and that other character who's related to Jimmy Swaggart—the "Great Balls of Fire" guy, Jerry Lee Lewis. That's Jimmy Swaggart's cousin. And the country and western guy down in Houston, Mickey Gilley, he's cousin to them both. And Sam Phillips developed their styles.

During this period I was doing a top-ten listing of country songs, the "Harry Gaines Top Ten, KTAE, from Central Texas." I'd send in the list of my top ten every week to *Cashbox Magazine,* and they would carry my hit parade. They'd use four or five more lists from around the country. Because of that, I gained a lot of popularity among country and western artists who wanted to get their names on that list. They were always visiting our area, anyway.

One time Sam Phillips called me and said he had this fella he wanted to bring into Texas to promote, and he wondered if I'd be interested. I said, "I guess so; what did he record?" He said, "Folsom Prison Blues." That's how I ended up booking Johnny Cash for two shows in Austin. We did okay, if I remember right. Earlier in the day he came into Austin, and I got him in to Price Daniel, the governor of Texas, who gave him an honorary degree from the University of Texas. Then we drove back to Taylor and I interviewed him on my show. Johnny Cash was more popular than Elvis Presley at that time.

You could see that Elvis was coming on, but when I called the guy from the Dessau Dance Hall and told him I wanted to book Elvis Presley again, he said, "I'm not going to book that son of a bitch. I had him before and I lost on him." So I called another friend of mine and got the show booked into a place called the Owen Davis Sports Center in Austin, a place where they had wrestling and other sporting events from time to time. It held maybe three hundred people. This time, the deal was that I was to get 20 percent of the gate.

Elvis came to town driving a pink Cadillac, and the mobs of young people—seventeen, eighteen, nineteen years old—who came out to see him tore the hubcaps off. He had a chrome rack across the top and they tore that off, too. When he pulled up, people just swarmed the car. We had to have a half-dozen police officers escort him down to the dressing rooms, to get him away from the public. And he didn't even pull up in front of the building; he was on the side. It was during the show that the fans stole the hubcaps and ripped off the rack.

On that same show we had Johnny Horton as the second feature. This was before he sang the song, "North to Alaska." Johnny was quite popular at the time, though, and since we really couldn't be sure how well Elvis Presley would draw, we felt Johnny Horton was good insurance. We figured Johnny would pull even if Elvis didn't. It turned out just the opposite. Elvis Presley had arrived. He had eclipsed Johnny Horton, and no one would ever again make the mistake of wondering if Elvis Presley could fill a hall.

I didn't have as much contact with him the second time as I had the first, so I couldn't really tell you if he'd changed in between as he began to get popular. I emceed the show and introduced Elvis that night. The funny thing was—remember this is a sports arena—

the stage was a boxing ring, so I climbed into the ring to do the introductions. In a way, I was introducing the next heavyweight champion, I guess.

We had the first two shows, and after the second show I wanted to settle up with Horace Logan. I went to him and said, "Okay, I want my cut. Let's work out the finances here."

He said, "We don't owe you but $170."

I said, "A hundred and seventy? What are you talking about? It's supposed to be $1,200 or $1,400." We'd sold $7,000 or so in advance tickets, and my take should have been closer to $1,400.

I said to Horace, "How do you get that?"

You know what he said to me? "Twenty percent of the gate — that's what came in the door. We didn't mean the advance sales."

I said, "Well, look, if that's the way it is, we won't have any more shows. We'll cancel right now. Your third show won't go on."

Horace did not receive that suggestion in very good humor. He said, "If you do that, I'll ruin you. You'll never be able to do anything in show business the rest of your life."

I was a young person at the time, and I took him at his word. So we had the third show.

Elvis was a hit the second time I booked him. He was out on the stage shaking himself around and blasting out the songs. As disc jockeys like to say, he was number one with a bullet.

The crowd was just shouting and cheering and wanting pieces of his clothing. You know how later in his career, when he made his comeback, he'd throw those scarves out to the ladies in the front rows? Well, even then, he'd throw his handkerchief out there.

I had a great time. It was wild. I was having an ego trip myself. Here I was, as a local radio personality, introducing all these stars. But I knew that Elvis was going to become a big star.

To this day, Elvis Presley owes me $1,400. Not that he's in a position to pay . . . unless all those *National Enquirer* newspaper stories are right, and he's still around somewhere, hiding.

I'll tell you one thing: he's not hiding out along the Kenai River. I would have smoked him out by now.

Change of Career

I finally got back to fishing a little bit in 1958, but, boy, that wasn't the biggest change for me. I quit the radio and became a policeman and moved to Hobbs, New Mexico. That's right, I became a cop. Actually, I wasn't giving up the radio completely because my first job was as a dispatcher. Different kind of radio, for sure, though. You didn't interview Elvis Presley on that radio station.

If you recall, I had made a change to become a news reporter for NBC in Florida, but that became a dog-eat-dog kind of situation where it was hard to get ahead. I didn't really have the proper schooling, and I had speech deficiencies. I had a southern accent. After all, I am from Texas, and I never worked hard to change my voice. Even now, on the radio and television newscasts, everyone has a neutral voice, like they all come from the same place, but you're not too sure where that place is. One place it isn't is the South, though. I was getting jumped on for that, for having a southern accent. It was something I was born with, and I couldn't retrain myself. It wasn't even that thick an accent. Of course, you can't hear me. You'll have to take my word about that. I wasn't fired from my job or anything, I just got tired of the system when it didn't seem like I'd be able to get ahead.

I looked around at other announcers at the time and saw where they were getting assigned and where they were going. That was the reason I was in Florida, because of the way I sounded. They wouldn't think of putting me in Washington, D.C.; they wouldn't think of putting me in Philadelphia. My options seemed limited. I just didn't sound universal. And about that time, my friend John Cameron Swayze began having some problems with the network.

He was the one who got me in there and helped me. Things change in any business. Groups follow groups: the buddy system.

It was time for a change for me. I was making $40,000 or $50,000 a year, expenses paid, with a vehicle furnished, when I jumped to police work for $350 a month. A *month*. It was quite a financial change. In the six years I did that job, my salary rose to only $425 a month, and I had a sergeant's rank. I was a police officer, and I eventually became the civil defense coordinator for the city, the NORAD representative—that's the North American Air Defense Command—going around making speeches about getting your air-raid shelters built. I got no money for that.

You know, when you're a kid, you want to be lots of different things. Well, I was trying out lots of different things. I chose Hobbs because my sister and brother-in-law lived there, and there was a job opening in the department. At that time there were about 30,000 people in Hobbs, and the police force had thirty-two officers. Hobbs had a small-town atmosphere, but it was a wild community because of its location. We were a stopping point for the hoods and thugs who frequented Las Vegas and the Dallas–Fort Worth area. These were burglars and safecrackers, not gangs like you see today. Individuals. You know, gambling and robbery kind of go together. There were transient laborers, too. It was an oil industry town with a lot of rough businesses surrounding it. Lots of people in and out. Short-timers. On Saturday nights we'd put twenty-five or thirty people in jail. Just a typical Saturday night.

As records and identification coordinator, I catalogued the information brought in by the police department detectives, a couple of investigators from the sheriff's department, and one or two state troopers. I kept the complete file. I was the central clearinghouse. So that everybody could know what was going on, there was one location for all the information.

One time there was a murder we were having trouble solving. The murder occurred right across the street from the police station, in a dentist's office. The dentist was murdered, and we considered robbery to be the motive. We immediately established a task force. We got the break in the case at the C. R. Anthony store, which was like a J. C. Penney's. This place was a one-floor retail department store with a balcony at the rear. The offices, directly above the shoe department, were on the balcony overlooking the store. A manager overheard one of the shoe department employees talking to another person about the murder and about what they were going to do. The manager heard only bits of what they were saying, but he called the police station and reported it. The call was referred to me and I assigned someone to check it out.

It turned out that one of those people was involved in the murder and was later found guilty. He was a young man just out of high school, but while he'd been in high school we'd become quite familiar with him. He was a rabble-rouser. He'd get drunk and start fights and was constantly brought to the police station. You could almost predict on certain nights that he would be a customer.

We'd call his parents, and his mother would come down, and she'd say we were just picking on him, that there was nothing wrong with him. And that's how he turned out. He was a murderer.

Another interesting case involved a series of armed robberies. Someone was robbing convenience stores and service stations.

Most times, almost immediately after a robbery happened, a local reporter would show up at the station wanting to know the details. He had to be monitoring a police radio. He'd be the first one at the station, wanting to know what happened. We'd sit there in the office, and we'd talk. He'd get the information from me and write a big story for the newspaper the next day. He wrote detailed stories about this epidemic of robberies, lots of description. This went on for several months, robbery after robbery and story after story.

Finally, the reporter left town. He moved to Albuquerque, where he got himself a job on a bigger newspaper. And lo and behold, shortly after he went there, he got caught pulling an armed robbery. Then he confessed that he was the one who had committed the armed robberies in Hobbs. He had done it for the benefit of having good stories to write, if you can believe that.

It was quite a change of life-style, becoming a policeman after all those years in radio. I missed radio, though I was doing something I enjoyed. Sometimes there would be singers coming through town who would do country and western shows, people like Webb Pierce. We were friends, and whenever they came to town, I'd make it a point to go down to the theater or nightclub to renew our acquaintance. I missed the glitter and the glamor and the atmosphere, but I never came close to getting back into radio as a career. That was it.

It was very enjoyable to get back to fishing, though. I started doing it again for the relaxation, and because I had the time again. But it wasn't very convenient to fish in Hobbs. There wasn't much nearby at all.

I'd drive about sixty miles to Carlsbad to fish the Pecos River. Sometimes we'd go to a small man-made lake a little ways out of Hobbs. A bunch of the guys would do it for recreation, to get away. I was still far from realizing that I could combine fishing with making a living.

We'd catch catfish and sun perch in the river and trout in the lake. These were fish eight, nine, or ten inches long. We'd go for a weekend or on a day off. Not that often.

One other important thing happened during my life as a policeman in New Mexico: I met my wife, Dorothy, whom I call Dot. In a sense, I'd been fishing. My sister introduced us — this is 1964 — and we went out dancing. My brother-in-law was playing in the band that night. About six months later Dot and I got married.

Not long after that, I decided that my career as a police officer had run its course. This was late 1964 or early 1965, I believe. The pay was low, and there was no avenue to make any more money, so I quit and went to Las Vegas.

You always figure there's big money to be made there, one way or another. I went there to be a security guard at one of the hotels, and I got a job at one of the biggest — Del Webb's Mint in downtown. Most people's perception of Las Vegas nowadays is formed by the Las Vegas Strip. It's the Strip that's grown up and where they have all the new hotels and where they have all those big-time boxing matches.

It was exciting there. There's something about Las Vegas that gives it a special aura. Maybe it's just that it's this city in the middle of nowhere, in the middle of the desert, and it never sleeps. It's a twenty-four-hour town with lots of action, a different world, really, from other cities in this country. There's nothing like it. Downtown Las Vegas is a street of neon. It's colorful and bright. There are so many lights that even in the middle of the night it looks like it's the middle of the day.

My job as a security guard meant that I spent a lot of time protecting people who had won a lot of money. You had to see that they made it back to their rooms or to another hotel, wherever they were staying, without being harmed by anyone. Casinos are notorious for attracting people who might watch others win money and then try to take it away from them as soon as they move away from the crowds.

That's pretty bad publicity for a hotel. It's one thing for them to actually beat the house and win the money. The occasional winner is good for a casino, as long as he doesn't win too much, anyway. It spreads the reputation around that a player can win. In the long run, the casino might actually win more money back from people who think it's easy to win there than it lost to that one big winner.

Basically, we watched people who won $5,000 or more. We considered them a security risk. And not just from people who might rob them. You know how you see in the movies that crowds gather around tables when someone is hot, when they're on a run. Well, that does happen. We were also protecting them from people who suddenly wanted to be their friends and suggest ways they could spend their money.

It was kind of fun being a security guard in a place like that, but the job didn't really seem like it was going to lead anywhere, either. So after about there months I went back to Hobbs and got into retail work at Clark's department store, the first of many I worked at. I did make more money than I had as a police officer, about $750 a month, but that still wasn't very much compared with what you could make elsewhere in the country, and you weren't going to make that much in Hobbs even if you were managing the store.

But retail sales, working for big department stores, turned out to be the career that put me on the road to Alaska. Not without another stop or two, but without that change I might never have moved to Alaska, never have moved to the Kenai Peninsula, and never have become a fishing guide.

For one thing, I certainly learned how to sell.

Alaska, At Last

Deep down, I'd always had a desire to go to Alaska. It wasn't the place to go if you wanted a career in radio on the national level, or if you wanted to be in show business, but the other part of me, the part of me that loved the outdoor life, always thought Alaska was the place to be.

I'd read a lot about Alaska. I'd followed the news when it became the forty-ninth state in 1959. Alaska had been in the news quite a bit. I read *National Geographic,* too.

It was the thought of the hunting and fishing that tugged at me. I'd read books, even though I'm not a big reader. Just general stuff. Not Jack London. I'm not one of the many people who came to Alaska because they grew up reading Jack London.

Even though Alaska isn't nearly as wild as it used to be, and even though it wasn't that way in the 1960s either, it still had the image of being the last untamed place in America, a place where you could still go to establish yourself and make your fortune. It was still the Last Frontier.

I probably never thought much about Alaska until I was older than a teenager. But it really crystallized as a place to go during the congressional discussions about statehood in the late 1950s and when Alaska was accepted into the union.

I was still a young person then. I'm still a young person. I got excited about it because it was the first time the number of states was going to be expanded in my lifetime. The other thing that got my attention was that this state was going to be bigger than Texas. I don't think Texans have ever gotten over that.

As I said earlier, I wasn't exactly striking it rich in the department store business at Clark's, but I did feel you could make more money doing the same thing in other parts of the country.

But I didn't go straight to Alaska. I'd heard that Seattle was the place to be because it was an excellent market. They had Boeing, and there was a boom in the airplane manufacturing industry. It was growing fast. So I left for Seattle with the family in 1969, and I landed a job almost immediately with Valu-Mart stores. They were the first major discount department stores on the West Coast. I worked in a Valu-Mart store in Bellevue, a suburb of Seattle, and within a three-month period I built that store from eighth to second in sales among their twenty stores.

Marketing and merchandising, that's the secret. It always has been, whether I was selling door-to-door, selling singers, selling myself, or selling the Kenai River. At all times I've been marketing and merchandising, persuading people to buy something. My philosophy is you can do anything you want to do. You've just got to apply the principles of salesmanship to it.

It's hard for me to outline those principles in detail. It's just something that comes naturally to me. It's not a point-by-point plan. I'd say it's an extra sense, realizing what people will buy and what they won't buy. And being willing and able to obtain that product, in the hopes that they'll buy it.

Merchandising is putting the product in the proper display, where people will buy it. One case I can remember involved ladies' hosiery. Okay. You have it on a shelf, and you've got it marked at 99 cents, and it just sits there. But if you take it and put it on a table, put it up by the front door, and put up a sign that says, "Regular $1.99 — Half Price 99¢," then it will move. You're actually getting the same price as when it was on the shelf, but it's the merchandising that gets people's attention. Part of it is psychology.

Anyway, by building up the sales at my store so quickly, I got the attention of the higher-ups. They found out who I was in a hurry, and they were impressed. It was good timing because they were considering opening a store in Anchorage. They approached me and asked me if I'd like to move to Anchorage, be part of the management team and operate the store.

It was January 1970 when I came to Alaska. You can always tell the people who really wanted to come to Alaska, who came with the serious intention of staying, because they came in the winter. Alaska is an easy place in the summer, but the winter involves a commitment.

When we moved to Anchorage, we committed ourselves to an apartment that wasn't built yet, so for about the first six weeks we lived in a hotel, the old TraveLodge. The company paid for it.

The store wasn't complete yet either. They were still building it, and I was going through the routine of planning the interior, ordering the merchandise, and eventually putting the pictures on the wall. You can't just throw the doors open and say, "Come on in, folks, we're here." It takes a lot of work and a lot of people to put it together.

While all of this was going on, we had one of our first real Alaskan experiences. We learned really quickly what cold can be like in Alaska. Remember, it was February.

When you're just commuting back and forth between the house and the store, you don't take much care in putting on layers of clothes, and you don't take notice of how cold it really is. You know it's cold, but it's not noticeable because you're not outside very long.

Anyway, every February in Anchorage they have an event called the Fur Rendezvous. It goes back many years; it's a throwback to the old Alaska days. The trappers used to spend all their time alone in the bush catching animals. Then they brought their furs to town for auction all at the same time and had a good time partying. The Fur Rendezvous is a modern version of that.

There are lots of activities — there still is a fur auction — including sporting events and the World Championship Sled Dog Race. They start the race right downtown on Fourth Avenue. Most of the winter they plow the streets to keep the roads clear, but for the race, trucks full of snow drive in and dump snow on the ground so that the dogs can have a smooth track. There aren't too many places where you'll see something like that.

Since this was our first time in town for the Rendezvous, we were fascinated by everything, especially the sled dog racing. We all went down to Fourth Avenue to watch the races, the five of us.

Here it is twenty degrees below zero — that wind whips right through downtown when it comes off Cook Inlet, which is wide open to the north — and the way we're dressed, we must be thinking it's winter in Arizona, not Alaska.

Our association with winter was held over from Seattle. Last I heard, Seattle doesn't have minus-twenty-degree weather. Dot, the kids, and I are standing there on the side of the road, wearing tennis shoes or sandals and freezing to death. I mean we were cold, miserably cold. But we really wanted to see the event, so we stuck it out. That's the day we realized we had better buy some winter clothes for Alaska. We went on a shopping spree. We equipped ourselves with boots, coats, hats. After that, we were ready for a blizzard above the Arctic Circle.

Just in the way I had to learn that winter in Alaska would be different from any other winter I'd experienced in my life, I had to learn that summer in Alaska — and fishing in Alaska — could be different from any I'd ever experienced, too. Guess what? Summer in Alaska is not summer in Seattle, either. Or summer in New Mexico. And there's definitely no connection between summer in Alaska and summer in Florida or Texas.

That first year, I decided to visit the Kenai Peninsula to go fishing with a couple of other guys from the store. It was my first visit to the area. Now, February or March is almost spring in much of the world, but not in Alaska.

One thing I can remember very clearly is that there was still a lot of snow on the ground. The whole area surrounding the Kenai River is heavily wooded, and in parts there are some pretty good-sized mountains. By that I mean 4,000 or 5,000 feet high. The snow stays on those mountains into June, for sure, and in some spots longer. It was a heavy snow year.

We brought a three-man tent and sleeping bags with us, and we spent the night near Cooper Landing, which even today has only a few hundred people. The tent was erected on top of the snow. It was a little old dome tent, real thin. We were cold, but not that cold.

The next day we drove on down to Kenai, which is about another sixty miles south on the Sterling Highway, and we went fishing. We didn't know the river at all, didn't know the best places to go. And we certainly didn't know that the best way to fish was from a boat and not from the riverbank.

This is how organized we were and how much investigation we had done: wherever we saw the river through the trees, we'd pull over, duck under the tree branches, and start fishing for a while. We'd cast out, rear back, and throw our arms forward, as if we were tossing a football. We had little lures on the ends of the lines that wouldn't have attracted any fish anyway.

Naturally, we didn't catch anything. Over time, of course, I learned that you don't fish that way, and you definitely aren't going to catch anything with that method.

It wasn't that we were hoping to catch a king salmon, specifically. We would have been satisfied with anything at all, anything that might bite.

Some time Saturday, on this weekend trip, we made it into Kenai. There was so much snow piled on the side of the road that it looked like a snow city, like buildings had been sculpted out of the snow. That winter the snow was measured in feet, not inches. I don't think we had as much snow as that again until the winter of 1989–90. Maybe one other time. It was quite impressive, that first time when we drove into Kenai.

Kenai has about 6,500 people these days, but it was smaller then. The first people in the area were Kenaitze Indians, but the Russians set up a trading post in 1791. There is still a Russian Orthodox church in the town and a lot of Russian influence all over the region. Kenai celebrated that heritage with its bicentennial in 1991.

We spent a second night in the tent, over on Swanson River Road, a popular recreational area now. It was cold that night, too, colder. On Sunday we drove back to Anchorage without any fish to show for the trip.

Still, what that trip did for me was plant the idea that there were lots of places to go fishing not far from my home, and after that first fishing trip I started going off looking for them. I'd take off and fish at Lake Louise near Glenallen, Nancy Lake near Willow, in small lakes around Wasilla, and at several streams on the Hatcher Pass Road, between Palmer and Willow. All over. You can drive to all those places from Anchorage in a couple of hours.

Not that I was catching anything on those trips. I was striking out. But I was having fun. It wasn't until later in the summer that I finally started putting the activity of going fishing together with getting fish.

Fishing for Fun and Profit

In 1971 people just didn't realize how great fishing the Kenai River was, what big fish you could find in it, and how to go after them.

That was the year I moved from Anchorage to Kenai. I joined the Carrs grocery store chain and left the big city for a fishing paradise. I didn't really know it was a paradise, either, but I did recognize that I could go fishing there all the time.

I bought a small boat, and I began to fish the Kenai River. It was about a twelve-foot boat, nothing fancy. When I first started fishing there, you never saw a tourist or never saw one that you really could bet was a tourist. When I went out fishing in those days, you were lucky if you saw seven or eight boats on the river in a day. All day.

I got set up on some river property on the Lower Kenai River that I turned into my fish camp and that I fish from to this day. It's about seventeen miles from the mouth of the river. At first I leased the property, two acres with five hundred feet on the river itself. It was still very rustic, with nice trees, but the bank was rough, eroding. It was just a place to go and fish from and spend a little time for recreation. You should see how much the banks have eroded since then. I buttressed the shore on the edge of my property with old automobile tires and large rocks.

Dot and I bought a trailer. We bought it in Anchorage, towed it down the highway, and put in on the property. That's still there today, too.

During that first summer we had a lot of barbecues. A lot of friends would come out, and a few of us would go out and fish. I think that first year or two we probably had more fun enjoying the

Just me and my shadow. You like the likeness? This wood carving of me lives at the fish camp facing the Kenai River. (Photo by Lew Freedman)

outdoors, enjoying the barbecues, and enjoying the people than we did fishing because we didn't really know how to fish.

When I first bought the boat, I originally thought of it as something I could haul around to use to fish the lakes. And I did do that. There's quite a few lakes on Swanson River Road that we went to for catching fish. These were lake fish, little lake trout, anywhere from eight or ten to twelve inches long. That was about the only thing we could catch on those lakes.

That boat was okay on the lakes, but the Kenai is a little more turbulent. The Kenai is not a raging river, by any means, but it has a steady current of three to six miles an hour, and we had to watch out for boats with large motors coming by. We could get swamped.

The boat was so small that it was like a bathtub. It wasn't even a big bathtub. It was dangerous on the Kenai. The gunwale was only a few inches high. When you sat down, the water was right up near the edge. People hesitated to get into it. Only two people would get into it at a time, myself and one more, to go fishing.

When we went fishing then, we also used heavy rods, the kind you'd use to go halibut fishing. Halibut can weigh three hundred pounds or more. In fact, the state record is something like four hundred and fifty pounds. Those fishing rods might as well have been baseball bats. That's how much overkill they were. They were really stiff, and what you need to catch king salmon is a flexible rod that will bend and give when the king begins to run. A strong king can snap a stiff rod.

But we didn't know that at the beginning. We thought that the king salmon was a big, heavy fish, so we needed a big, heavy rod. We would use what's called a teaspoon lure. The lure had a triple hook on it, and a four- or five-inch flapper that revolved like a big motor as it went through the water.

We used lead above that, maybe two feet above the lure, two or three ounces to drop the line to the bottom and keep it there. The one thing we did know was that salmon were bottom fish. So we were ready to go whale fishing. Honestly.

The boat would drift and the hooks would constantly get caught on the rocks. We were hung up more than we drifted. Everything was just so out of balance. The boat, the rod, the lures, everything. We kept catching the bottom. We had great success at that. The lead would hang up between rocks and stick there. Or there would be some trees down, and we'd hang up on them. We would spend more time getting ourselves out of these predicaments than we would fishing. This went on all year and into the next year, too. Occasionally, we might have caught a fish.

They were big fish but not big kings. We'd get twenty-five or thirty pounders. My first year, though, I bet I caught more kings just casting off the bank from the fish camp than I did in a boat, especially early in the season.

Not that it didn't take some patience. I used a lure, with a large treble hook, that was fluorescent orange on one side and had a regular chrome finish on the other side. I'd have to cast three, four, or five hours before I'd catch a fish. I'd cast across the main stream, the deepest part of the river, just kept casting, back and forth, back and forth, just cast, cast, cast. How to build strong muscles twelve ways.

Sooner or later those fish would come through, and I'd hope they were hungry for a snack. When they came through in a school, I'd hit one, maybe two. It was sporadic, but if I waited long enough and worked hard enough at it, I'd get a king from the shore. Back then that was the recommended way to catch kings.

I talked about fishing a lot with my friends, though at that time most of my fishing was on weekends or days off or when I could slip away from the Carrs grocery store without Larry Carr knowing about it. A lot of my friends decided they wanted to go fishing, too, and I started taking them out in the boat on the river.

Finally, it dawned on me—why don't I start taking people out fishing and charge them?

Considering that there weren't many people out fishing regularly, this didn't seem like an automatic road to riches, by any means. One person who did receive national recognition for fishing the Kenai and for guiding on the river, just about the only one who predates me as a guide here on the river, is Spencer DeVito. Spence really developed a lot of knowledge about the river and the fishery—how to get kings and the right equipment to use—and he was free with his advice. He was generous with that knowledge.

The stereotype of the fisherman is a guy who jealously guards his best fishing spots, the type of bait he uses, the type of gear he uses, and what kind of fish he finds at his favorite fishing hole. But Spence wasn't like that at all. He didn't mind telling you how he did things, and at one time Spence operated out of my property. He was a guide, too, independent of me.

Spence was probably the first commercial fishing guide on the Kenai. I'm sure there are other people who claim they guided people here prior to 1970, but I don't think they can make much of a claim. To me, a professional guide is a person who goes out and advertises, sells his services, and proves himself worthy and professional. I don't know of anybody who was doing that besides Spence DeVito before I was.

There were some older people around who fished the river, some old-timers who went out, but again very few who even took a boat out, never mind guided anyone. Phil Ames was one of these.

Spence was out there early, before people truly discovered the river, before the tourists started coming up in heavy numbers, and before guides began appearing out of nowhere and calling themselves professionals, even though they had no real knowledge of the river.

He eventually got turned off by the whole scene, the growth and expansion of fishing and guiding, and stopped doing it. He still fishes a lot, but he travels all over the world trying to catch different species. He fishes in Hawaii and Mexico. It's a different world, a different kind of fishing. I occasionally see him, but not with clients on the river.

By 1971 or 1972 we knew we had to develop different ways to catch the fish. It just wasn't practical, and not as much fun, to be out on the river all day, spending half your time tangled up, not fishing. It kind of increases the odds of catching something when you have the line in the water.

The great experimental stage began. We early fishing guides began to try to build our own lures. We'd buy little Okie drifters, which are round, one-inch or two-inch bobber types with holes in them. We'd use different colors. We'd put a treble hook on. Then we'd put the lead on.

We tried several different, what you'd call sophisticated, methods to go for the fish. One method led to another until we got it down to a real science. This was over a long period of time. What was done was fine-tuning a system with the best rods, the proper bait, and the right planning, so that fishing for kings is now simple, and almost anybody out there has a good chance to catch one.

Almost anybody. Catching kings still isn't a snap. You need the cooperation of the kings, and there's some luck involved. The fish has to be in your neighborhood at the right moment. There are a lot of people I know who live in Kenai, near the river, who have lived there ten, fifteen, or twenty years, who tell me they fish the river religiously, year after year after year, who still have not caught a king.

I know two or three people who've been on my boat and come every year, fishing once or twice a year, who still have not caught a king. Everyone else on the boat will catch a fish and they won't. It just happens that way. Nobody's perfect. That's why I always say that if you catch a fish, you have to consider yourself lucky.

The fishing rods we use now are so different from what we used initially it seems as if they're not even in the same family of gear. They are light. You can balance them on your finger. They weigh around six ounces, that's all. The material used to be fiberglass, but now we use graphite and other complex materials. They're much lighter, but they can take more abuse than ever. I've got rods that you can bend into a complete circle. That's important. They have to be sturdy and long-lasting because a lot of people use them day after day, and many of those people are novices, so they tend to be harder on them.

Where we used to use fifty-, sixty- and even seventy-pound test line, we're now using twenty- or twenty-five-pound test line. The poundage of a test line does not exactly correlate to the poundage of the fish you're catching. The breaking strength of a line is judged by the weight. If you buy a twenty-five-pound test line, the breaking strength on that line is twenty-five pounds of tension. It should break at twenty-five pounds.

That does not necessarily mean the biggest fish you can catch with that line weighs twenty-five pounds, which is what a lot of people think. The world-record fish, caught by Les Anderson, weighed 97¼ pounds and was caught on a twenty-five-pound test line. See, the secret is that a line is about ten times as strong under water as it is above water. For example, you could probably pick up a two-hundred-pound rock under water with ease, but if you found it on the bank, you couldn't pick it up. It's the buoyancy.

We were using seventy-pound test line when we started. To realize how silly that sounds, that's almost as strong a line as you would use for halibut. We thought, "My God, fish that weigh eighty pounds!" and we'd think, big rod, big line.

As for the lures, over the years we went from teaspoons to the Okie drifters, to Spin N' Glos—the little plastic bait hooks of many colors we use now to actually catch the fish.

We were always side drifting, too. That's all we did up until the late 1970s. A side drift is when your boat is drifting sideways down the river, and everybody's dragging a line out of the same side of the boat. But if you're drifting sideways, you drift only so far, and then you take your lines out of the water, start your engine, and go do it all over again. So half the time the line isn't in the water. There are still some fishermen on the Kenai who enjoy drifting, but we've developed another method that is a little bit more scientific. That's using the engine for back trolling.

In back trolling we're sitting with the lines out the back of the boat, we're holding the current. We're drifting with the current, and the boat is holding steady, too. The line is in the water 99 percent of the time. We don't constantly have to move the boat back upriver. The chances are greater of catching a fish because the line is in the water longer.

One of the advantages of fishing out the back of a boat while trolling is the ability to avoid getting the lines all tangled up. You can separate the lines better. I used to have to cast all of the lines out by myself with side drifting because people are not really familiar with doing it properly. We would drift and tangle, and that would be a hassle. Sitting in seats and trolling, you can put one line out to one side, one line out to the other side, and one farther out the back of the boat on each side, above the motor. The lines are let out at different distances. One guy's out a little bit, and one guy's out quite a bit.

Another reason I prefer trolling is that you have more of an opportunity to catch a fish because you're introducing the bait more directly to the fish. As he is migrating upriver and you're back trolling, you're dropping the bait right in front of him. In the side drift, you're going downriver with the current, and if the fish sees the bait, he has to turn around and swim to it to catch it, instead of just grabbing for it. He has more time to think about it, and it takes more effort, so it lessens the odds of his making the move.

I know of very few occasions when a king salmon will accommodate you by jumping into the boat when you're not even trying. Unless you're my friend Bob Penney, who is chairman of the Kenai River Sportfishing Association.

Early one season he was out on the river in his boat, and he had a couple of other people with him. Well, kings will roll. That means they jump slightly out of the water. They get frisky and break the surface. Some fishermen think that's just to tease them. Well, this time the king jumped so high, it jumped right over the side of his boat and into the net on the floor of the boat. How's that for a ready-made catch? Special-delivery salmon.

That's not the only time I've heard of a king actually beaching itself in someone's boat. One time a few years ago I saw it happen. Rick Richards, who is a taxidermist in Soldotna, was fishing at Eagle Rock when someone in his boat got a fish on. I just happened to be looking in their direction. Everyone in Rick's boat reeled in and let the fisherman play the fish. Well, the king came out of the water one time. It looked to be about a thirty-pound king. It came out of the water a second time. And the third time it broke the surface, it jumped right into the boat. Saved Rick the trouble of netting it.

It happened so fast, the people in the boat were all startled. And so was I. They were just standing there goggle-eyed, looking down at the fish. There were all those boats around, and a lot of people must have seen what happened because you could just hear the laughter in the air over the river.

I couldn't believe it. I said it out loud, "I don't believe that." I was thinking, I can't believe that's happening. Why doesn't it happen to me?

Then the clients in the boat started asking me, "Can we do that? Why can't we do that?" It put a lot of pressure on me to live up to something like that.

Strange things do happen when you're out fishing.

About two years ago this fella landed a ninety-three-pound king salmon, the biggest fish taken that year. He was fishing at Sunken Island, which is just upriver from my fish camp, and he got a hit.

The fish ran and struggled, and he knew it was a big one. The fish was so strong it broke his line. He immediately repaired it, put a new lure on it, and got another hit right away. This fish felt just as big as the first one, though the odds were against it. This one he hung on to, though, and brought it in after a good fight.

Believe it or not, when he reeled it in, he saw his first hook caught in that fish's mouth. He caught the same gigantic fish twice. It was just a mean, aggressive fish. The same fish twice. Amazing.

You know, most of the lures we use on the Kenai River probably have been tested with bass in the Lower Forty-Eight. They've proven good for bass, and we adapt them slightly for salmon. They seem to take to the same kind of lure.

Bass are generally a smaller fish, but there are some parts of the country where they get up to twenty-five or thirty pounds. I know someone who lives down here on the Kenai Peninsula who has a striped bass that weighs over sixty pounds mounted on his wall. It was caught in New England, off Cape Cod, I believe.

A king salmon is a more aggressive fish than a bass, more aggressive than most game fish going for bait, except maybe the smaller kinds of trout. You might say that if trout were people, they'd be habitual midnight snackers who don't know to stop when it's good for them.

Going back to the bait for a minute, whenever we used those colored hooks, we were also using salmon eggs. From the very beginning, we recognized that the eggs from salmon themselves were the very best bait. Over time, we've salted them and used netting on them, wrapping them tightly together, or used rubber bands to get them bunched. Elastic bands worked really well so that the salmon eggs didn't come loose in the water. Now I use a regular bait-holder hook. The hook itself has a line that slips down on the shank and forms a loop that you can actually set the bait into.

The first couple of years of taking people out on my boat on the Kenai was basically a freebie situation. Looking back, I was developing myself, figuring out how to be a professional guide. I knew what the potential was, what the possibilities were. I just sensed that it was something that was right for me, and right for the area. Maybe all of my years of selling and marketing and merchandising let me see it, even if there really was no market at the time. It's like going into a community and saying, "Is there a chance of putting out a newspaper here?" The market's there. It was just something that hit me.

The first couple of years were trial and error. I was mainly catering to local people and some people from Anchorage. It wasn't until 1974 that I began my advertising. By that time I had another off-season job, working for another store.

My present rates are $125 for a half day of fishing on the Kenai River. Initially, I charged $25 and we'd go out and spend the day if we had to. As a matter of fact, I had one client who came up in 1974 and spent two months with me. He loved to fish and wanted to stay out all the time. That was how I met Dean Yeasel, who became my close friend and business partner.

In fact, that's how I got a new boat. Remember how that old one, the twelve-footer, was so unstable? Dean is a businessman whose company manufactures plastic products in Ohio, though he spends part of his time in North Carolina and now Alaska, too. He didn't like going out in the old boat. He didn't like it at all. He had very little faith in it. He figured if he was going to be nervous all the time, he couldn't have a good time. He could have bought his own boat, but he didn't have any way to transport a boat back home, so he bought a new one for me and spent all his time in it.

There were huge differences between the two boats. The old one just had a bench across it, no fancy seating, and was steered from the stern. The new one was a sixteen-foot Monarch with a steering wheel, and it was much more stable. Dean said, "It's yours. Just take me fishing." He even came out with other clients.

That was the end of my first boat, my bathtub. Today you couldn't even use that old boat because there's so much traffic on the river, it would swamp you before you got comfortable.

Even I was afraid of that little boat.

Zero to Sixty in Nothing Flat

From nobody fishing the Kenai River to thousands of people fishing the Kenai River seemed like it happened overnight.

There was nobody guiding. Just Spence and then me, and it all mushroomed with a little bit of advertising. People really began to come into the area, and that brought in a lot of other guides, too.

They were publishing newspaper stories about me in Washington and Oregon and California, and the first thing I knew, the guides who normally work down there during the winter months decided to come up to Alaska during the summer. They saw the opportunity to make some bucks when it was off-season at home. It happened almost instantly.

Well . . . by instantly I mean over four or five years. By 1978 I could see we were going to have problems with people on the Kenai. And I don't really mean the volume of fishermen as much as I mean the guides who showed up. Fly-by-night operations.

Ninety percent of the guides were from outside Alaska. They'd come up here just for a short summer or not even come up at all. There was a time when people outside the state were selling trips to the Kenai Peninsula and wouldn't even show up. It was fraud.

The customers — fathers and sons, businessmen, people who had planned for their once in a lifetime trip — would come up to Alaska, and there would be nobody to greet them, nobody to take them out on the river. It was bad.

They'd come to Anchorage or into Kenai, and they wouldn't be able to find their guide service. A lot of them would call me up and ask if I had heard of such and such a person. I'd say I didn't know him, and they'd tell me their story about how they'd hired him and paid him for a trip that didn't exist now.

In many cases I ended up taking those people out on the river. I don't know how many times I did that. I know Spence DeVito did it, too. And there were probably other Alaskans around who did the same thing. We did it to save our own reputations and the reputation of the Kenai River.

Those people were getting ripped off, and if we didn't take them out, they would have gone home and bad-mouthed us all. Word gets around fast. We would have all been tarnished. It might have ruined our whole industry.

Those people would have gone home and said things like, "Oh, the Kenai River. I went up there and got taken for a ride."

We felt we had to defend ourselves by taking them out fishing. We actually started working through the Chamber of Commerce. People would call them to complain, or they would call me because I was listed in the phone book as a guide. Sometimes the Chamber would call me, asking if I'd heard of a particular guide. I'd hear the story and work the clients into my program. It had to be done. If I didn't have room for those people, I'd call somebody else and see that they were taken care of.

That was a very risky period. It could have set us back for a long time or permanently.

When that kind of thing started happening we legitimate Alaskan guides knew we had to get organized. Spence DeVito and I contacted the Coast Guard. The Kenai is a navigable river and it comes under their jurisdiction. They weren't really enforcing any rules there, though. It just wasn't a high priority at that time.

That was the beginning of the implementation of a lot of rules, but at that time there were no rules governing who could operate a boat and no procedures for licensing guides.

In 1979 we persuaded the Coast Guard to send someone down to Kenai and give an examination to the existing guides working the river. We had between one hundred fifty and two hundred people show up. That's how fast the guiding had grown. Incredible.

Back then it was just a brief test, and although it was felt that some regulation was warranted, the Coast Guard didn't want to be in the position of putting people who were trying to make a living out of business. It wouldn't have been fair to step in and say, "You've got to do this, this, and this, or find a new way of life."

Now, though, there is a very demanding test to get your boat licensed and to be licensed as a guide. To put a boat on the Kenai now you have to have navigation equipment, lights, communication capability. You have to know a lot to get a Coast Guard license.

After the first test we organized the Kenai River Fishing Guides Association. Then we started getting involved in political issues.

There have been a lot of changes on the river since the first time I guided a few friends around the neighborhood.

One time back in 1974 or 1975 when I was demonstrating boats for Northern Commercial, I had a new boat with a fifty-horsepower engine down at my place along the river. It was a new model, and I needed to test it. So Dean Yeasel and I got into the boat and went downriver. I was wearing a suit and tie.

Right around the bend, within a mile, there's an island smack in the middle of the river. We got just out of sight of the camp when the engine conked out. The boat drifted close enough to reach the island and we got out.

Dean and I were stuck there for about four hours before anyone else came along whom we could wave down to give us a ride back to the fish camp. If someone got stranded there now, there would be somebody there the minute after it happened. And there would be somebody watching from the bank and laughing, too.

On the busiest days of the summer, there may be six hundred or seven hundred boats out along the Kenai River. That sounds remarkable, but there's plenty of room. It's a big river. The problem is that they all congregate in the same few places, instead of spreading themselves out.

They all want to fish at Beaver Creek. They all want to fish at Eagle Rock. They all want to fish at the big eddy. Those are the best-known landmarks on the river.

Eagle Rock is just a big rock that you can see at low tide sitting in the middle of the river. It's a big, big rock, about twelve feet tall and probably about twenty feet wide at the base, which is under water. It's definitely going to stay there. Beaver Creek is just below Eagle Rock. It's a creek coming into the river. Just another distinguishing feature along the Kenai. The big eddy is where a big bend in the river creates churning water.

I think people like to say that they caught a fish at the big eddy because it sounds good. Or they like to say that the fishing was hot at Eagle Rock. I say it, too, when I give my fishing report on the radio. But you can catch fish anywhere along the river if you spend the time and effort. The fish go only in one direction, and that's upriver. It's moving around and taking your bait out of the water that's going to hinder your chances of catching fish.

I move during a fishing trip if there's no action, but I'm only moving within a three- or four-mile area. You shouldn't be moving all the time. If you are, you're going to miss the fish. Then again, a lot of people like to do boat rides. I don't. I like to go fishing.

What's the best spot to catch salmon? I think you can develop your own spots anywhere you want on the river, just like I have. I know where the channels are. Some of them are near my fish camp. That's how I got the nickname Quarter Mile Harry, because I've caught so many fish right there. My chances of catching a fish are just as great there as ten miles downriver. Those fish have got to come through.

To be truthful about it, though, Eagle Rock may be the very best place. People like Eagle Rock because it's closer to the mouth of the river than those other places I mentioned, but more importantly, the fish are more concentrated in their schools coming through there. They're in a big group. It's only after that that they split up and move up the river singly or in groups of five, six, or ten.

Yet the time span for catching a fish is shorter at Eagle Rock. When they're concentrated like that it helps your chances of catching a fish, but the peak time may last only thirty minutes.

Farther upriver, the fish split into smaller groups and may be passing by for as long as three hours. You can fish the same spot — and the same group of fish — for that long.

You have to be patient to catch fish. You know the image of the lonely fisherman just sitting and waiting out in the rain on a lakeshore all by himself. Well, you don't have to be lonely, and you can have a good time even if you don't catch anything, but the bottom line is true. You can spend a lot of time out there chasing fish. You can spend a lot of time being outsmarted by the fish.

Even if you know where the fish are and where the fish are going to go, and even if you have all the right equipment and are with a knowledgeable guide, it's possible some of those schools of king salmon and silver salmon have really been to school and earned a diploma. They may be too smart to take the bait.

All my years on the river and all my experience just contribute to evening the odds.

Repeat After Me

"Okay, ready to go?" I asked. That got the clients' attention. Those were the words they wanted to hear. I was sitting at one end of the boat, on a seat behind the console and the steering wheel. The women were looking back at me from a couple of feet away, definitely ready to go — ready to catch king salmon.

"Raise your right hands and repeat after me," I said.

The women in the boat — friends from two different towns in Alaska — raised their right hands, just as if they were being sworn in to testify before a jury.

"I solemnly swear I will not jerk my rod when I feel a fish bite," I said.

"I solemnly swear I will not jerk my rod when I feel a fish bite," they repeated.

"If I catch a fish, I'll tell the whole world who I caught it with," I said.

They laughed.

"If I don't catch a fish, I won't tell anyone who I fished with," I said. And I winked.

Everyone laughed.

That took care of the administering of the Harry Gaines Oath.

In my early days of guiding on the Kenai River, back in 1971 and 1972, I always wanted to give the people who came fishing with me a good introductory speech. You know, wake them up, put them in a good mood. But the first boat I had was so unstable that safety was the main thing on my mind. I didn't want people standing up, falling overboard, and suing me.

I wanted to make them laugh and put them at ease, but my first welcoming speeches were probably a bit on the dull side. I probably sounded more like a stewardess telling people to fasten their seat belts and observe the no-smoking signs than I did like a stand-up comic.

I wanted to set a tone of light-heartedness and enjoyment, but I probably came off as solemn as a civil defense coordinator. I think people's eyes tend to glaze over when you give them safety run-downs, even if they know it's important. But over time I developed the oath, and I think it lets me hold people's attention. Then I can slip in the safety information when they're not looking.

It was early afternoon on the Kenai River, just after lunch, and it was pretty quiet. Guides were starting up their motors for the second fishing trips of the day and were ready to cruise downriver to their favorite fishing spots. We were going after king salmon, one of the world's greatest sport fish.

The sun comes up early in mid-June in Alaska—it practically never sets around the summer solstice in most parts of the state—and it had been beautiful all day. I had already had one group out starting at six in the morning and back in at noon, and I was going out again from one to six o'clock in the afternoon. That's when the river shuts down for fishing during king season. I had two women in the aluminum-hulled, flat-bottomed boat that is provided to me by Coca-Cola.

There was Susan, sixty, from Anchorage, and her friend Tami, thirty-four, from Nikolaevsk, and they were planning to make a citizen's arrest of the biggest king salmon they could find. Our half day of fishing on the Kenai was a birthday present for Susan—and an anniversary present for Tami—from their husbands.

These people were out to have a good time and it was my assignment as their paid fishing guide to make sure they did. They also wanted a fish to take home for supper and I was going to do my best to make sure they got that, too. There's nothing like the taste of a fish being barbecued in the backyard when you've caught it yourself. I should know. I've been catching salmon on the Kenai River for over twenty years, and I never tire of cooking my dinner when I've brought home the bacon. There's something special about that—a feeling that you worked for your dinner, just the way people at the beginning of time did.

A fishing trip on the Kenai River—chasing king salmon—can be for both sport and food. It can be fun, and it can be work. The only promise that I make is that a fishing trip with Harry Gaines will be fun. The work part comes in if you catch a fish and it doesn't want to cooperate. Not many of them do. They're not meek fish. They're rather emphatic in their desire not to join you in the boat.

I've had celebrities from all areas of show business and the sports world come out fishing with me. I've had people from all over the United States and the rest of the world come fishing with me. These are people from all walks of life—doctors, lawyers, businessmen—and I have a good time with all of them.

Most people bring the proper attitude with them when they go fishing. They're hungry for a fish and good-natured about spending the time it takes to get one. Susan and Tami just happened to be two fun ladies who wanted a king salmon caught in Alaskan waters, but they knew how to have a good time, too. I love having people like that in my boat. There's no sense being dour. We're going to be out there together for five or six hours. My attitude is let's all be pals.

I could tell early in the trip that this day of fishing would be a pleasant one. Susan announced, "Here we are, Tam," as she dropped her fishing line into the water and raised her face to the sun's rays. "Our husbands are working their butts off and we're down here playing."

Susan then looked over at me, squinted a little bit, and said she wanted to know if the fish had been telephoned, heralding her arrival.

"Did you call them?" she asked. "Did you tell them Susie is here?"

"Ho, ho, ho," I answered, which most of the time passes as a pretty good imitation of Santa Claus.

I always like to say I talk to the fish, so I guess she was testing me, making sure I had kept the lines of communication open.

Well, it must have been a very clear connection that day because not fifteen minutes out on the river, while we were still in sight of my fish camp back on the bank, Tami's rod was bending. You could tell right away that it wasn't caught on debris or anything. She had a fish.

"Reel in!" I shouted. "You've got a fish on."

Susan reeled in her line.

Tami reeled in her line too, though not quite as fast, because she had something struggling on the other end. About two minutes later, Tami had the fish up next to the boat, and I netted it for her. It wasn't a king salmon, though, but a sockeye salmon — a red. It was an attractive fish, about seven pounds, but definitely not a king. The king salmon these ladies had come for are at least five times that big, and they were hoping for one even bigger than that.

I put the fish down in the back of the boat. It wasn't dead yet, and it kept squirming, so I grabbed the metal club I keep hanging from the console and bopped it on the head a couple of times. The club is called a Kenai Konker and it's advertised for Whopping Big Fish. You know something — it works. A couple of hits with that and the fish stopped moving. I would have been quite surprised if it hadn't. The konker is about as reliable as a policeman's billy club. Even if Susan and Tami didn't catch anything else, they would have dinner waiting to be cooked.

"If there are reds in there, there's got to be others," I told them.

It's exciting when someone catches a fish. That's what everyone's there for, and it charges up the atmosphere. Once one person catches a fish, it seems to energize everyone else in the boat. It livens up the mood.

The funny thing was that we caught that fish so close to my fish camp. I can't tell you how many times that's happened. That's how I got the nickname Quarter Mile Harry — we've caught so many fish within a few hundred yards of my property. I guess the fish just naturally come to me. I must have a magic touch. (Actually, I wink when I say things like that.)

Susan took a long look at Tami's dead fish.

"Want me to show you how to do it again?" Tami asked her.

Zing! I chuckled. A lively crew.

It was 1:30 in the afternoon, time to check in with the radio station, KCSY, 1140 AM. Time for a live fishing report.

I carry a transistor radio in the boat and turn it on just before my hourly fishing report starts so that I can hear the end of the last song and wait for my introduction from the disc jockey. I could hear his voice on the air: "In a moment, we'll check in with Harry Gaines."

As soon as we came on the air for the live fishing report, I put the microphone in front of Tami.

"What's your name?" I asked.

She wasn't expecting it. You could tell that from the look on her face. But she answered just the same.

"What'd you catch, Tami?"

"A sockeye salmon," she said. She was proud and beaming.

"We were looking for king salmon, but we caught a sockeye salmon as a bonus," I told the listening audience. "This is Harry Gaines on the Kenai River. We'll be back later."

I like to think of my fishing reports not only as informational but also entertaining. It's a short version of "Prairie Home Companion." This is "Alaska Home Companion" — folksy and friendly.

Most of the time the report lasts only a few minutes, and sometimes when I interview people who caught fish, it lasts only a few seconds. But we can talk all afternoon if we want to. I'm capable of it. And I'm willing. One day I'll see if the radio station will let me. Maybe I'll let them play one record an hour and I'll talk for the rest of it. Reverse the lineup on them. I could talk all day about fishing for king salmon.

I'd say, during a good season, about fifteen hundred people come fishing with the Harry Gaines Guide Service, and I never get tired of it, mainly because I meet new people every day. I get just as excited over that new person catching a fish as I would if I had caught it myself. It never gets old. I may have caught a lot of fish, and a lot of people may have caught fish with me, but it's always a kick when someone catches their first fish. It's special for them, and it's a treat for me to see them enjoying it so much.

It turned out that our early joy with catching that red salmon wasn't a signal of great fishing for Susan and Tami. A couple of hours later we hadn't even seen another fish. Sometimes it goes like that. The fish always have the ability to throw you off guard. You'll be sitting there in placid waters thinking nothing's going on, and then there'll be an explosion of activity. The fish will begin biting so fast, you'll have a couple of people in the boat with fish on simultaneously. Or you can go a whole day and never have a fish even bump your rod.

We heard a rumor from someone in a passing boat of a king that was caught around a bend in the river, but nothing was happening for us.

I don't know if it improves the odds of catching a fish or not, but after awhile you've got to assume they're running through a different channel and move on. We packed the rods into the boat, turned up our collars, and put the throttle down to speed to another spot.

Even in the summer, when the sun is strong, it can get cool on the Kenai River, and when the boat is moving the wind is strong. My beard is long enough, and the wind is strong enough to part it in half as we go. The beard flows out to both sides, onto my shoulders.

We found a good spot between Eagle Rock and Beaver Creek and brought out the fishing rods again. Those women really wanted to catch themselves a king. It wasn't hard to find a comfortable place, because it was a slow day on the river, with only about fifteen boats in the area. On busy days there'll be hundreds. We've got a different kind of gridlock than you'll see in New York City, and it seems strange to see crowding on a wilderness river, but it does happen when the fish are running strong.

The fish come in groups, and this was just not one of those days. Susan was becoming really worried that she would go home without a king salmon.

"It's even gotten to the point where I wouldn't care if you caught a fish," she said to Tami. "It's that desperate."

I decided we needed a new strategy here to wake everybody up.

"Are you talking to the fish?" I asked them.

Well, the second I said that, Susan got a bump. The fish hit hard, and she knew right away that this was the real thing.

"Come on, Susie's fish!" she screamed.

She wound that reel fast. Some people don't hold the line tight — they freeze or yank back on the rod — and the fish gets away before the hook is set.

"Keep reeling. Keep reeling," I told her.

I reached for the net and kept an eye on her to make sure she didn't jerk the rod. She remembered her oath, though, and was doing fine.

"Just take it easy. He's a big one, I'll tell you that. Just keep your rod pointed in one direction. He'll keep going in a circle. You're doing good."

Susan was having a grand old time. She was giggling and squealing, but she never lost sight of her basic task. She kept reeling, bringing that fish home. That woman had a very specific goal.

When the fish broke the surface of the water close to the boat, I leaned over with a net and scooped it up. Then I quickly threw it to

See the way the wind parts my beard? We get some breeze on the Kenai River when we've got the throttle open. (Photo by Lew Freedman)

the floor of the boat so that it couldn't wiggle out of the net. The fish flopped and trailed blood from its mouth as Susan stamped her feet and whooped. She was one happy lady.

"Wow!" she yelled. "I never caught a fish like that. See, that's what they look like, Tami!"

I brought the club out again and gave the fish a couple of swats to put it out of its misery, and it expired. When we weighed it later, it weighed in at twenty-seven pounds. That's a big fish by most standards, even if it's not large for a king salmon. Not that Susan cared. She was just as thrilled as all get-out to catch one.

When everybody was back in their seats again, I led a fish cheer. "F," I said, "I, S, H. What's that spell?"

"Fish!" they shouted back at me.

"Louder!"

"Fish!"

We hadn't been sitting there but a minute when Susan started gloating about her catch to her friend, teasing her and making jokes about its sleek, silver flanks and impressive size.

I don't know when I've had a better prospect for the radio, so when the time rolled around for the next fish report I put her on the air.

"Tell me, what did you do a little while ago, Susan?" I asked her.

"I caught a great big king salmon," she said.

Then she proceeded to tell the whole Kenai Peninsula how she'd landed this big fish and how her good friend Tami—poor thing—hadn't caught one.

Her good friend wasn't about to let that pass. Tami reached over from behind and grabbed a big piece of Susan's leg and pinched her. Susan screeched, "Ouch!" and we were all laughing so hard we could hardly sit up. This was all on the air.

Dan Donavan, the disc jockey, was on the other end, wondering what was happening, but he didn't miss a trick either.

"Thank you, Harry Gaines, for another scintillating report from the river, squeals and all," he said.

I guess you'd have to classify that trip with Susan and Tami as a great moment in fishing history and also as a great moment in show business history.

That was just an average day on the Kenai River, fishing with Harry Gaines. The moral of the story is that you've got to come fishing with me because you never know whether you're going to make your mark on history.

All Clients Are Created Equal—in Theory

The best client I ever had was Dean Yeasel, since he became one of my best friends.

I still remember the time Dean decided he was going to take me fishing. This was years ago. When you're a fishing guide, guiding for king salmon, it's illegal for you to fish at the same time as the clients. The rules are different for silvers late in the season. Then it doesn't matter. You can trail a line out the back of the boat with the other fishermen.

But when you're guiding for kings, with the hours on the river being limited to 6:00 A.M. to 6:00 P.M., you never have the opportunity to catch a fish yourself. So one day Dean said he was going to take me fishing.

We got out on the river, and before too long I hooked into a king, probably forty or forty-five pounds. A good-sized fish, but not a super fish. Now Dean is—how shall I say this—an oversized man, and he doesn't have great maneuverability. His maneuverability is kind of sloppy, in fact. He doesn't even like to stand up in a boat. He doesn't balance that well.

Well, here I am with a king on the line, and I'm fighting it and trying to draw it up next to the boat. We were gaffing the kings back then, not netting them, so I asked Dean to get ready to stick the fish. He got the gaff, but when he lunged for the fish, he missed.

He was supposed to aim for just below the dorsal fin, spear the fish, and come up into the boat with it. He'd seen me do it many, many times, and I knew he was capable of doing it.

When he reached out for the fish, though, he was a little off balance, and instead of jabbing the gaff into the fish, he hit my line. He cut the line clean through and the fish escaped. A clean getaway.

I couldn't let this pass. I made a big issue out of it. I pretended it really upset me, even though I really just wanted to burst out laughing. I pretended I was really mad and demanded that he take me back to the fish camp immediately. I was saying things like, "If you can't do any better than this, take me back to camp, and I'll hire myself a guide."

So we get back to camp, and I'm being real theatrical about all this for Dot's benefit, just making a fake scene of it all. I didn't know where it would all lead. We got out of the boat, and I'm showing off, and I throw the rod and reel up on the bank like I'm disgusted. And wouldn't you know it? The reel broke right off. I broke it by being silly and stupid.

Did I say that fish was forty-or-so pounds? Nah! It must have been a world record. Remember that rule — if it gets away, it was the world record. I suppose I had the last laugh on him, though, in a way.

We were in the boat, drifting down the river, and Dean was using his brand-new rod and reel. As a matter of fact, his wife, Phyl, had just given him a golden Dawai that she'd paid $129 for. And this was some time ago. It was top of the line. It was gold-colored, a very nice piece of equipment.

Now Dean likes to talk, and sometimes he likes to take a break from fishing when he's talking. So he parked his rod — his new fishing rod — in the rod holders on the side of the boat, but he left the line hanging over the side, still in the water. I was sitting back at the console behind the steering wheel, and Dean spun around in his chair to face me so that I could hear him.

I could see what was happening behind him. The line got caught up on a rock or something else on the bottom, and he was hooked. But Dean was talking ninety miles an hour. I was trying to butt in and get his attention. Finally, he asked me what was wrong, and I told him. He spun around in the chair and reached for the rod, but by then, with us drifting, and the line tangled but good, the drag on it was so tight that it wasn't giving at all.

Just then the line got so tight that it actually pulled through the rod holder and broke it, and all the pieces — the rod holder, the rod, and the reel — went right over the side into the river.

It was the first time Dean had used the rod. He was going out of his mind. We spent an hour, or even longer, in that spot dragging an anchor along the bottom of the river, trying to catch the line and salvage the rod. Up and down with the anchor, over and over again. But once something goes over the side into the river, it's gone.

It was not a happy trip for Dean, going back to tell his wife.

Not all the clients I take fishing on the Kenai are like Dean. I do have a lot of regular clients who come up to Alaska and fish four, five, or six years in a row with me, and I also have clients who fish with me once and then show up again ten years later. That happens almost every year. It makes me believe I must have done a good job the first time, or they wouldn't be back.

During the summer of 1990 I had a woman out fishing with me who was twenty-four. She hadn't been fishing with me in seventeen years. Her daddy brought her out when she was seven. She came out with a friend, and you should have seen how thrilled they were when they caught one. That was something, to see how much time had passed. She was a little girl and now she's a grown woman.

Still, you've got to advertise for clients, find ways to bring new faces to Alaska and to the Kenai year after year. I have advertised in magazines, with travel agents, and with my own picture cards placed in stores, hotels, and the like around the state and all over the world.

If you're going fishing with Harry Gaines, we're going to make it as easy as we can for you. We supply experienced guides. Besides myself, there are several other guides for our busiest days. We supply power boats, all fish cleaning if you catch anything, and all the gear you need to catch a fish. That's tackle, pole, reels, and bait. Plus free coffee.

Also, since I got Coca-Cola as a sponsor a few years ago, we have free Coke on the boat. Diet Coke, too. At one time Pepsi sponsored me, but Coca-Cola made me a much better deal. Every year they give me a new, four-seat aluminum boat. Those are the most comfortable boats I've ever had. The seats make you think you're in the living room, settling in for a football game.

There's no way that I—or any other guide—can guarantee a customer a fish, but I do my best to keep a client satisfied anyway. They'll ask questions, and I give them the answers. That way they feel they've learned something and gotten something out of the experience, even if it's raining the whole time and they never see a fish. The show must go on. I guess I learned that early enough in life when I was touring with that horror show.

One of the most frequently asked questions I get is, "How deep is the river?" It's not a deep river at all. It's not deeper than ten feet. They'll ask where the river gets its green color. That's from the glacial melt. And they'll ask how fast the current goes. It moves at up to six miles an hour.

These days people marvel at the bank erosion, too. On the high side of the river there are a number of houses where the bank has receded right up to the back porch. These will probably have to be abandoned or moved, if possible, within the next few years. There used to be thirty feet of soil between the homes and the river's edge, but time has eaten it up. There are trees you can see half standing, or tipped over, whose roots have been washed out. Some of those trees fall into the river.

When I first started guiding on the Kenai, my introductory speech was more safety-minded. That was probably because even I didn't trust my first boat, so I thought it was important to make sure the clients thought about safety. I would give the people a little lecture, telling them they had to have their life jackets on. We went through a little ceremony putting them on. Some of them were Mae Wests. They bulge way out. You remember Mae West . . . she was sort of like Dolly Parton, if you know what I mean. That was kind of the opening for me to tell a few jokes, and that's how I warmed everyone up. It was like being the master of ceremonies for a stage show.

Then I'd show them how to operate the boat in case something happened to me. Remember, there weren't nearly as many people around then to come over and help out on short notice as there are now, when the river gets crowded.

I try to tell new jokes every year. Sometimes I buy joke books to keep my material fresh.

Over the years, with thousands of clients, maybe twenty thousand to thirty thousand in all, I've had all kinds of people. People kind of classify themselves for you right away—put themselves into categories.

The first thing a lot of people say right away is, "I've never done this before." So I say to myself, "I'm gonna have to do everything I can to help them." I know I'm going to have to explain everything. I want them to feel good about what's happening, not feel lost. I enjoy doing that. I'd rather take a person like that fishing than someone who's been fishing a lot and acts like he knows it all.

All clients are created equal, but some require a little more atten-tion than others. (Photo by Ken Graham)

The know-it-all doesn't really need me. I try to let him do his own thing, but 99 percent of the time he's asking for my help before it's over.

Then I've had people — a man and wife, for example — and she gets a fish on and he doesn't. Then he tries to tell her exactly what to do. It's her fish, though. Sometimes I have to be a little bit aggressive (though only in a joking fashion) and say, more or less, "Just sit your butt down over there. She's got the fish on and we're gonna catch it." But I've got to do it in a way that's not offensive to him.

I don't mind fishing with the person who thinks he knows it all. What I won't tolerate, though, is him telling other people what to do. I've had to tell people to be quiet and remind them that the client is paying me. I'm the guide here.

When we start cleaning and bagging the fish some clients say, "What are you doing?" What I'm doing is putting the salmon eggs aside to keep and use for bait. We provide all the bait for catching fish, and that's one way we get it. But there will be fishermen who say, "Those are mine. They're out of my fish."

It's customary for the guide to keep the salmon eggs. Most of the time I'll negotiate for them if the question comes up. At one point a few years ago, I put up a sign that said the eggs belonged to the guide unless prior arrangements had been made.

You might wonder why clients would want the bait; there are two possible reasons. They might want to use it themselves to fish some more, or they might want to eat it. People do eat raw salmon eggs.

I've tried them. What do they taste like? Fishy. Surprise! They're very rich in taste but kind of oily. They're okay. You might mix them with another food, like rice. Even if you don't cook them, you soak them in salt water before eating them. They're sort of like sushi.

Every trip is different.

The perfect illustration of how you never know what to expect is the time my mother came up from Colorado to visit and went fishing with me. This was about 1980 or so when she was seventy-two or seventy-three years old.

My mother was just relaxing, sitting out on the boat launch, fishing for Dolly Varden. She was using the smallest hook that you can purchase, with a single edge on it, a quarter-inch hook, and using six- or eight-pound test line . . . not a very strong line at all.

Before you know it, this king salmon came along and grabbed the hook and swallowed it. Don't ask me what that king was after. That was like finding a thimble in the desert. But as small as that hook was, the fish was hooked. My mother got excited, and she was hanging on even as the fish began to tug and run. While she was gripping the pole, we managed to get her off the launch and into a boat, and we went around the bend drifting with the fish. She couldn't fight it too hard because the hook couldn't have been in very deep, it was so little.

Just seeing the fish from a distance I knew it weighed sixty pounds. It had to. It was a big fish. I also knew that if I didn't gaff it when it first broke the surface, it was gone. That hook and that line weren't going to hold. If I didn't hit it just right we could wave bye-bye.

Well, the fight went on. We'd gone perhaps a quarter of a mile downriver when the fish came up right alongside the boat. I reached down to gaff it and I got it just below the dorsal fin. I had the gaff in and I started raising it up and up, lifting the fish into the boat. Right then I thought we were going to get it. My mother was next to me, and just then she slipped and went over backward and fell onto the floor of the boat.

I was still raising the fish, but the floor was wet and slippery, and I fell down, too — blam! on my butt. The fish was partially into the boat . . . it was that close. But the gaff came out and the fish went overboard.

There was no rhyme or reason for why that fish was caught, and there was no way it should have gotten away at that point. But she did catch it, and it did get away. It just wasn't meant to be taken. That fish got lucky and got its freedom.

Just another fisherman's tale about the big one getting away. There's a million variations on that theme, right?

Some Real-Life Fishing Adventures

Not every fishing trip is a success because you catch fish. Some trips are successful just because you survive them.

In 1975 I had one trip far from the Kenai River that began with good intentions. With my buddies Dean Yeasel and Richard "Doc" Breece—a friend from Sidney, Ohio, who really is a doctor—I headed out on a four-day trip to Twin Lakes. That's a remote area about two hundred miles west of Kenai, across Cook Inlet.

Our first problem occurred before our plane even left the ground. When we had loaded our gear the plane was too full. We looked around and there were still piles of things on the runway. We had obviously planned on having too much fun. Still to be packed were gasoline and a motor for the boat we were going to use on the lakes, as well as our case of liquid refreshment.

We looked at each other and we looked at the things piled up on the runway. No contest, right? So we packed the liquid refreshment and left the gas and the motor in Kenai. Just how we thought we were going to get around the lakes I don't know, but it seemed like the right choice at the time.

We got out to the cabin, set up our beds, and made ourselves comfortable. That night, the very first night, Doc woke up and yelled, "Get out of here!" And he kicked this weasel clear across the room, twelve to fourteen feet. It flew across the cabin and landed on my damn bed.

That was just the first weasel. They were all over. They followed us around like dogs, and they got into our food. Weasels, bah!

This was a sturdy old log cabin. It had slits for windows, and the door was a good two feet thick. It was bear-proof. But every day outside the cabin we would see some bear scat. There were definitely bears in the vicinity, and that made us nervous, because they may have been lurking in the dark scouting us out for future meals. If any of us got up to pee in the middle of the night, the others would be sure to go, too. As if safety in numbers would really help against a grizzly bear.

We fished in the lake, but we weren't catching anything at all. We enjoyed our liquid refreshment, but before long we finished almost all of it.

Then thick, gray clouds rolled in on us, and it became pretty obvious that our plane wasn't going to be able to come in and get us. Our four-day fishing trip turned into a five-day trip. Then six, seven, and eight days went by.

You know what we caught in eight days? One humpie. And we ate it.

Food became a problem. We hadn't been planning to establish residency at Twin Lakes, though with all the gear we had you would have thought we'd brought enough provisions to outfit an army. We decided we'd better hunt for food.

Dean shot a squirrel, and I cooked it up in a stew. Just as I was cooking, a plane flew over, and we got all excited. The plane broke through the clouds, and we figured we were on our way home. We began packing up the gear and for some reason those guys dumped the pot with the stew. There was only one problem — it wasn't our plane. It flew away, and there we were with squirrel stew all over the ground — and nothing to eat.

Twin Lakes is teeming with wildlife. The sky was thick with Alaska Jays, birds they call camp robbers. They were the most easygoing birds I've ever seen. They weren't scared of man at all. I could hold bread crumbs out in my hand and the birds would take them. They would even land on my shoulder, walk up and pluck a piece of bread out of my ear. It was something to see. Of course, that's where our bread went.

One day, Dean shouted. He leveled the rifle and took two shots. I didn't see anything. Whatever it was had disappeared into the brush. Dean said it was the biggest rabbit he had ever seen. He insisted it was three feet high or more. A three-foot-tall rabbit? What was it doing, masquerading as the Easter Bunny?

We did shoot some more squirrels, so we had something to eat, but the days kept going by, and we were still stuck there. It was September and it got pretty cold. It started to snow while we were there, and we were beginning to think we were going to spend the winter at the lakes. But on the eighth day the plane came back and got us out.

After we got back to town, Dean went to a barber shop and began telling everyone there about the biggest rabbit in the world. They just looked at him, and one by one they left, until he was the only guy there with the barber.

"Was that a shave and a haircut, sir?"

No one's ever believed him.

It seems like every trip I remember started out being for a day or two but then turned into some kind of endurance contest. That's the Alaskan wilderness for you.

In 1977 I was on what was supposed to be a one-day fishing trip to Moon Bay. That's about 150 miles south of Kenai, on Cook Inlet. The bay got its name because it's the shape of a half moon. You come in at an angle, and there are two rock walls face-to-face. You've got to come in at low tide because there's soft sand. You just set down there. That's the Alaskan wilderness for you, too. A landing strip wherever you can make one. Dave Diamond, our pilot, made one of the beach.

It's a tricky landing at the best of times, but Diamond couldn't come back to get us — he sent somebody else. The pilot came in too low and, sure enough, he nosed the plane into the sand and got stuck.

He was able to radio to Anchorage to tell them what had happened, but the word was that we couldn't get another plane — we'd have to spend the night. One minor problem arose, however. The tide started coming in, and there was the plane, stuck in the sand. You know what that meant. The pilot, my friends Jerry Meyers and Tommy Waterer, and I had to free the plane and move it in the dark. We worked on that plane for three or four hours. We tugged it, pulled it and shoved it — about 150 feet up the beach. That was more work than I've ever done in my life.

Then we had to make sleeping arrangements for the night. Counting the pilot, there were six of us, including my friends' wives.

There was a cabin nearby, and most of them slept in that. But we also found a piece of plywood and built a bonfire on the beach, and I slept out there with Tommy.

In the middle of the night I woke up and had to go to the bathroom, so I walked off a little ways. On my way back I was feeling pretty silly, and as I got closer to Tommy I started making these noises. Little grunts, little growls. Bear noises. I kept coming closer, grunting all the time, and did Tommy come alive. Wow. I never saw anyone come up so fast. He'd been sleeping with a club, and he came up swinging. He nearly killed me.

I'll tell you, I stopped playing tricks like that.

That same year, 1977, I was selling boats for a living and sometimes I'd take demonstration models out to test them. One time Dean and some other people were with me, and we took a thirty-foot cruiser to Kachemak Bay, just off Homer.

We parked it in a little cove, threw the anchor out on the bank, and went to sleep on the boat. Three or four hours after we went to sleep, I woke up—everybody woke up. The boat was tilting and we were falling out of bed. The tide had gone out and we were hung up. The anchor was now above the boat. The front end was high and the back end was in the water. The water in the cabin was just inches from some of the bunk heads, and we crawled through the hatch on the bow to get out.

That same summer, just a couple of weeks later, I took another boat down to Homer. Dean and I anchored the boat and pitched a tent on the beach. Soon the wind started to blow, and it started raining. It was blowing so hard we had to weigh the tent down with logs to keep it from blowing away. We went to sleep, and when we woke up there were three inches of water on Dean's side of the tent. He was sleeping in a puddle.

But this was the unbelievable thing—we looked out of the tent and the boat was drydocked! The tide was out. We were a good hundred and fifty feet from the water. We had to push the boat. Obviously, we hadn't learned much from our other experience.

I did learn something that time, though. After that I always brought a long rope and staked the boat to the ground. That way when the tide went out the boat went with it, but it stayed anchored.

Not that strange things don't happen closer to home, fishing on the Kenai River.

On one fishing trip I was with a bunch of friends on the river when I saw a big old bird out there, and I yelled, "Look, guys, an eagle!" It turned out to be a black sea gull. Yes, I know sea gulls and eagles don't look anything alike, but we do get visited by eagles on the Kenai River. They're very majestic birds and when I see them I get excited. They're so special to look at with their big wingspans and the way they glide so effortlessly. Anyway, those guys have never let me hear the end of it. Every bird that flies by they go, "Hey, is that an eagle, Harry?" "Nice looking eagle, huh, Harry?"

Boy, I can't say anything. But it did have a heck of a wingspan for a sea gull.

Depending on the time of year, we can see quite a few sea gulls while we're fishing for kings. Sometimes they're just a white mass where they gather on a sand bar. You can get pretty close to them because they're used to man and don't expect to be hurt. But sometimes they can be a nuisance.

Once, on a hot day in July, I had a guy sitting in the back of the boat. He was wearing a baseball cap to shield himself from the sun, but it was a wool cap, and it was so hot he finally had to take it off. It wasn't two minutes before a big sea gull came by and splat! It got him right in the forehead. I usually prefer laughing with my clients and not at them, but he did look pretty funny.

One of the most embarrassing things that ever happened to me was at the close of the fishing season back around 1982.

A good friend of mine, Bud Walters, a local insurance agent, brought some clients out. It was the last day of the king season. He built me up really big to these guys, trying to impress them. He kept telling them, "Hey, you're going out with the number-one guy on the river." Lots of stuff like that.

It's early in the morning and we're getting ready to climb into the boat. I'm saying, "C'mon guys, let's go." Everybody climbs in, gets themselves settled in the seats, and I get behind the console. Only then do I look around. There are no fishing poles. There's no gas tank. Everything is gone. Somebody had stolen everything in the middle of the night. Now that was embarrassing.

Those fishing rods had my name on them, too. Just like baseball players who have their own model bats. Just like a Louisville Slugger. Whoever stole them couldn't even use those rods.

I bet they broke them in half and threw them in the river.

Celebrity Fishing

The call came the night before. It was a friend of mine calling to say that Tom Selleck wanted to go fishing. The next day.

And he was there in the morning. I used to watch his show all the time—"Magnum P.I."—I was a fan. But I wouldn't have recognized him as Tom Selleck. It would have been difficult. He definitely wasn't wearing a Hawaiian shirt or anything like that. He was very quiet, somewhat shy. He wasn't at all talkative. I had to be aggressive with conversation to get him to talk. Eventually I got the idea that he was just relaxed. He caught a thirty-eight-pound king with me. And no, he didn't pull out a .38 to shoot it.

His show was still on the air at that time, but I thought we didn't have anybody out on the river recognize him at all. There weren't any groupies or anything on the dock. But later that evening I did have another guide, Rod Berg, call on the telephone.

He said, "Harry, did you have Tom Selleck on your boat today?"

I said, "Why?"

He said, "Well, I was fishing near you [and I recalled that he was], and I could have sworn that guy was Tom Selleck. He looked so much like him."

Somebody in his boat had commented on it, and he'd gone home and told his wife, and she wanted to know where Tom Selleck was staying because she wanted his autograph.

I said, "Look, he's already gone." I really think he was still there, staying in a local hotel, but as far as they were concerned he was gone. He just came, he fished, and he left. Evidently somebody else recognized him easier than I did. But you can't give away someone's privacy. I told them he left town.

It came out in the local paper a few days later that he'd been in Kenai.

You know, that was several years ago, and I still run into people— especially females—who want to know, "Which seat did he sit in in the boat?" Really. And they want that seat. I still run into people at the supermarket who say that the next time he comes they want to get his autograph.

Every girl in town says, "When he comes back, you'd better call me."

Once, I got a phone call that Lloyd Bridges was in Anchorage for a tennis tournament and wanted to go out fishing for kings on the Kenai River.

It was really at a bad time, though. There weren't any fish. It was between the runs, if I recall. I told them so, but they said he liked to fish and wanted to come down anyway.

And darned if he didn't catch a fish. It was about a thirty-pound king. He was a nice fella. We made small talk. He talked a lot about how much he likes to fish. Of course, I had watched "Sea Hunt," and I'd seen some of his earlier movies, so I would have recognized him on the street.

He stayed around and did some fishing on his own, too. He went out and fished around the bridge in Soldotna, about ten or fifteen miles from here, and he caught some Dolly Varden.

Lloyd Bridges was the first celebrity to go fishing with me, in 1976 or 1977, and it was kind of fun having a celebrity out on the river, though I never thought at the time I would end up becoming fishing host to the stars or anything. Eventually, I did start to think it would be good for business having big-name entertainers come out fishing. How could it fail to be when word got around?

It's something that clicks in people's heads when they start thinking about going fishing. They think, "Hey, didn't I hear about Lloyd Bridges going fishing down on the Kenai with some guide?" Then they start thinking about which guide it was, and pretty soon they make some phone calls, find out it was me, and book a fishing trip. People think, "Well, if it was good enough for Lloyd Bridges, then it is good enough for me."

It does stick in people's minds, and I use it to promote the guide service. But sometimes these celebrities will ask you not to tell. They want to be left alone to have a good time and catch some fish.

Danny White, the quarterback of the Dallas Cowboys, was another celebrity who fished with me. He was coming up to do some work with the youth group of the Church of Jesus Christ of Latter-day Saints — the Mormon church. Now I'm from Texas and I was a Cowboys fan. In 1983 everybody was calling the Cowboys America's team. Danny White was on TV more than Lloyd Bridges at that time. This was early June, real early June. That was another case of bad timing. No fish.

Most of the celebrities who come to Alaska have other business bringing them to the state and they can't wait around for prime fishing conditions. You tell them in advance the fishing is just zilch right then. But they want to have a good time and I try to see that they do, even if they don't catch a fish.

Danny White really wanted to catch a fish. He wanted to catch a fish so badly that after we tried in the lower river for kings, I sent him out on the upper river with another guide, Larry Suiter, a friend of mine. They went out and caught some rainbow trout. It was catch and release for rainbow trout, though. So he did catch some fish on the Kenai River, but he didn't get to take them home with him.

Danny is a very likeable person. We talked about boats. He owned an interest in a boat-manufacturing company in Tyler, Texas. I bet I have as much interest in boats as he did. I make my living in them.

Danny White is no longer playing, but to tell you the truth, I'm not so much of a Cowboys fan, the way they've been going the last couple of years. I mean, I've lost faith in those guys. I'm more of a Houston Oilers fan now.

Many people get the idea that celebrities are on a plateau above you, but I don't. You really learn up close that people of all kinds are just human beings who have a job to do, and they just kind of hit it in certain areas. They're just doing their job in life. They're no different from anyone else when they're on the river. Just looking to have a good time.

The one thing that's different is the preparation. You don't want it known ahead of time that they're coming down. You don't want them to get mobbed. You want to make sure that they can have a good time. You try to keep it low-key. You don't go around putting up signs saying you've got Danny White or somebody else out fishing with you. That way you keep them coming back. I've had some I can't even tell you about.

I took out the U.S. Olympic Committee when they came to Anchorage to make their report on whether they should bring the Winter Olympics to Alaska. Last I heard they don't have fishing for kings in the Olympics yet. Maybe they should. It might help Alaska get the games some year. I guess you heard, though — we didn't get them. They'll be in France in 1992 and in Norway in 1996. I wonder how the fishing is in France?

I also had members of the U.S. Ski Team out. They were downhill skiers. One was from Albuquerque and she kind of hooked on to my New Mexico connection and we wrote back and forth for a little while. And we did catch some fish.

Another sports celebrity I had was Graig Nettles, the baseball star. This was after he'd left the Yankees — I think he was playing in San Diego. The people who set up that charter didn't want anybody to know about his visit. He fished two charters with me, one in the morning and another in the afternoon. And no one knew he was here except one other guide, whom I told. And he didn't tell anybody either . . . until after Nettles left.

The celebrity I had the most fun with was a lady named Edna Skinner. Do you remember Edna Skinner? Think about it for a minute and see if you can place her. She was a regular on a television show, back in the fifties.

Now Edna Skinner was from the state of Oregon, and she fished with me for three straight years. She was close to eighty years old the last time she fished with me. She was getting up in years.

Edna Skinner was a hell of a fisherman. Or fisherwoman, I suppose. She was the kind of person you didn't need to tell what to do. She already knew what to do. She knew how to do it. Her way. That lady could catch king salmon. I think the largest fish she got weighed seventy-two pounds. That's a very good-sized king salmon. And she was a small woman, probably not more than 120 pounds herself. It almost seemed the fish was as big as she was.

She was really a very aggressive lady. When she hooked into a fish she was all over the boat and she was working that fish. You're supposed to stay calm and play the fish, but she covered some territory in that little boat. At that time we were still using forty- to sixty-pound test line. That was rope.

So there was little Edna Skinner wrestling a seventy-two-pound king with a huge rope. She could have used rope like that for climbing on Mount McKinley. People will fool you. You have an elderly lady on board and you think she might need help and she jumps right up and wrestles that big fish into the boat.

Oh, yes, do you remember Edna Skinner? She was the actress who played the next-door neighbor on "Mister Ed." The talking horse. Maybe she had a special ability to talk to the fish from all that practice living near a talking horse.

It seems like I've had a lot of football players come out fishing with me over the years. Now most of those guys were considerably larger than Edna Skinner. And larger than the biggest of the kings, too. That doesn't mean they caught bigger ones than Edna Skinner, though.

One year, during the summer of 1989, we had twenty-five members of the National Football League come out. They were up here for the Jesse Carr Memorial Golf Tournament in Anchorage and we loaded them all into boats. There were guys like the lineman Bart Oates and the Matthews boys from the Browns — Clay Matthews and Bruce Matthews — who are all-pros. No big-time quarterback or really famous players like that. They're all linebackers or linemen, so their names are very seldom used unless they do something sensational.

No matter how hard you try, though, it doesn't always work out exactly the way you planned it. My adventure with Kenny Rogers certainly illustrates that.

This was about 1986, and Kenny Rogers was in Anchorage, singing at Sullivan Arena. I was told Kenny Rogers and his entire band wanted to go fishing on the Kenai. You can either drive the 150 miles to my place on the highway or you can fly, and they got one of those commuter planes to fly them down. I went out to the airport to meet the plane. There were about fifteen people in this group — Kenny Rogers's personal manager and some friends.

They all came down, but Kenny didn't show. He went in another direction. He must have felt that fishing on the Kenai River was too public and he just wouldn't have a good time. He is a pretty visible guy with that gray and white beard and his size. He thought the word was out that he was down on the Kenai. Well, it was.

We had cars lined up and down the Big Eddy Road, the street my place is on, just because people thought he was going to be there. I had to run people off the property. I told them to stand in the street. I didn't want them hanging out all over my land, crawling all over my property. And he wasn't even there! He went on a fly-in fishing trip somewhere else. That was one way to beat the crowds. They sure weren't going to charter a plane to follow him.

But the band came and we limited out. We caught fish like you wouldn't believe. Forty- to sixty-pounders. All kings. Everybody was catching them. So we boxed up all the fish and boxed up the band in their plane, too, and they all flew back to Anchorage and had their show at Sullivan Arena that night.

Well, they were all bragging to Kenny about how many fish they caught and how much fun they had. They had their fish with them at the arena. He had apparently struck out—hadn't caught a thing wherever he had gone.

So at 11:30 that night—this was a Friday, the weekend, a busy time—I got a call that Kenny said he'd decided he wanted to come down to Kenai and go fishing tomorrow. Tomorrow was Saturday and I was full. I mean every boat I own was full. It was the height of the season. We had room for fish in the boats if we caught them, but no room for more people. Not even a small child. I said okay, be there, and I hung up and wondered what I was going to do.

Well, one thing that I was not going to do was give up the honor of taking Kenny Rogers fishing. I was told there'd be about ten or twelve people, that he'd be coming with his aunt, his uncle, his brother, his mother, and four or five other people who follow him around. You know, a few security people.

So it was 11:30 at night and I jumped on the phone and I farmed out a bunch of people who were scheduled for my boat. I didn't just borrow a boat, I borrowed a guide. Then I called my friend at the airlines and had him fly the Rogers party down. I finally got everything arranged—in the middle of the night.

I met them at the airport, brought them out to my place, and put Kenny Rogers, his mother, his brother, his uncle, and his aunt in my boat. I've got a video of it. We headed downriver. It took twenty minutes to get to the fishing spot. We made one drag, lines in the water, and Kenny Rogers's mother hooked into a fish. Now his mother was eighty-something years old, okay? She hooked into a fish.

She was sitting in the back of the boat and Kenny was in the front. I said, "Hey, get back there and help her. You can help her bring in the fish." She wasn't physically able, or she didn't appear to be. She was hollering for help right away. In the process of people switching around and all, the fish got off. It got away. So I said, "Let's go hook another one."

And Roy Rogers — not the one who was friends with Trigger; this one was Kenny's brother — says we should go in. Go in? We hadn't been there fifteen minutes. "Go in?" I said. "We're just getting started. There's fish here. We just hooked into one." "Well," he says, "Kenny wants to go." Kenny never said a word. His brother did all the talking for him. About the only time Kenny spoke at all was when I was bringing him in from the airport. I told him I had been a country and western disc jockey in Texas, where he was from, and he asked me a little about that. That was it. Otherwise Roy did all the talking for him.

So we headed back upriver. We had planned a lunch for them, too. Dot had gone out and bought all the necessary provisions for lunch and had it all spread out because I had radioed ahead and said we were on our way back.

Sure enough, when we got in people were beginning to come out onto the property again. Word had gotten out that Kenny Rogers was fishing for kings on the Kenai. The newspaper was there, too. Kenny said to me, "You know, this just takes the fun out of things. Get rid of those people."

So I walked over and said, "Folks, would you mind moving back to your automobiles, back off the property?"

Then Roy came up to me and asked if there was a rest room Kenny could use. I said sure, and I pointed to the outhouse we had and said, "There it is." He said, "Well, do you have another one that he can use?" I said, "That's the one everybody uses." He never went.

People were standing out on the street watching. We had this big spread for lunch. Kenny Rogers just gulped his sandwich and said he was ready to go. Not back on the river for more fishing, back to Anchorage. So I took them all back to the airport and off they went.

Later I found out that Kenny was having cramps, stomach cramps. He had an upset stomach. He really had to take a crap was what he had to do. It struck him on the boat. That's why he came in from the river so fast. But they never told me. It was his personal manager who told me later he had a stomach problem. That was my experience fishing with Kenny Rogers. Less than thirty minutes on the river.

But you know, I've got him on video and I use him in my advertising. Kenny Rogers fishing with Harry Gaines.

Over the years, I've had a lot of politicians come out, too — governors and congressmen and senators. Of course, I've had Senator Ted Stevens from Alaska and Congressman Don Young, our only congressman.

I've invited President Bush to come fish the Kenai River for salmon with Harry Gaines. George Bush is a fisherman. You always read about him taking vacations and going fishing in Maine and one time in Key West. It seems he's a hell of a fisherman.

I wrote to him through the Alaska delegation — they're all Republicans — soon after he got elected, and I knew they'd see that my letter got through to the White House.

I got a reply, too. They said that they had no plans in the immediate future to come to Alaska but that my letter and invitation were on file. If he did come to Alaska, they'd do everything possible to see that he would go fishing with me. It wasn't a promise, it wasn't a commitment. That sure would be a lot of fun, though. As far as I know, I'm the only one who's invited him. But that doesn't really mean anything. If he even comes to Alaska to fish he'll probably go to the bush.

In 1989 we heard that Prince Charles might come to Alaska. I immediately jumped on the telephone and called Juneau to issue a special invitation to Governor Steve Cowper — and Prince Charles, if he was coming. But he never came.

I jump onto a lot of stuff. That's how I get a lot of people. You've got to jump on things when you hear about them.

You know, with all this talk of Elvis still being alive, you'd think he might show up to go fishing one of these days. He does owe me for that concert.

Can't you see the headlines now? "The King Catches a King."

My Bit for Diplomatic Relations

It would be easy to say that fishing is a universal language. I know I used to think so, and as an optimistic guy — all fishermen have to be optimistic — I'd still like to think that way.

But once you've gone out fishing with groups where nobody else speaks English, you start to understand just what kind of difficulties those folks at the United Nations have.

The Japanese are probably the most difficult clients to take fishing, mainly because of the communication problems.

Now you might think that they wouldn't be able to book a fishing trip if nobody spoke English, but you would be wrong. How do I get them? I don't know. They show up.

I've developed a system for the Japanese. Had to. There are lots of Japanese tourists who come to Alaska, and that means they're a big part of the market. I've cultivated Japanese clientele for a long time. I have a friend, Richard Campbell, who had his Japanese mother write instructions down on paper for me, and I had them printed up on cards.

The cards are in English and Japanese/Japanese and English, so I also know what they say. They refer to life jackets and safety, and there are references to what you do when you get a fish on and to some of the things I do to help them bring that fish in. After all, I'm not going to be able to tell them what to do at the time in a way they can understand easily. There's a numbering system, one through ten, and I can point to the number. If you'd been out there with me a few times, you'd know why I had to develop this system.

A few years ago we had about fifty Japanese tourists come in on a bus, and we took them out fishing for silver salmon. I put four of them in my boat, and I asked Dean Yeasel to go along to help me.

Well, we were just starting out, just pulling into the current from the bank in front of my fish camp. I was at the wheel trying to get the boat into position and throw out the anchor. Dean picked up the rod and was just trying to show one of the Japanese fellows, with hand signals, what you do to let the line out. He was demonstrating. While Dean was showing him, boom, a silver hit—just like that.

Oh, they got all excited. It was just like a zoo on the boat. They're small people, but all four of them were in the back of the boat, in one spot, and the boat was tilting all to one side, and they were very excited, just having a blast bringing this fish in.

And so they get it in—I net it—and it's on the floor of the boat and one of them was using a word over and over . . . "Chonk! Chonk!"

So we put that one in the tub and a few minutes later another one caught a fish and he said, "Chonk! Chonk!" They were all excited and having a good time. I wanted to become part of it. The next one caught a fish, and so I said, "Chonk! Chonk!" And they gave me a real funny look, and they got real quiet.

We finished fishing and went back to shore at my fish camp. One of the Japanese guys took out his billfold, pulled out a $20 bill and handed it over to Dean. Dean said no, I can't take it, there's your guide, pointing to me. And the guy put the $20 bill back in his billfold, took out a $5 bill, and handed it to me.

Later on I called my friend—the one whose mother made up the cards—and asked him what "chonk" meant. It turns out it means "mine." So when I said "Chonk! Chonk!" they thought I was trying to take their fish. I'm lucky the guy gave me a $5 tip.

And I always considered myself a diplomat who could get along with anyone. Put me at the United Nations and I'd solve the world's problems by taking everyone fishing. Come to think of it, maybe if they did all their negotiating in a small boat they'd have to listen to each other.

Another time I had some doctors from France who showed no sign of knowing English. Everything was in French, including their squeals of excitement. Even those sounded different from American squeals.

Those guys were experienced fishermen. They just wanted the opportunity to catch a king salmon on the Kenai River. They had been around the Kenai already. They did some fishing on the Kasilof River—from the bank—and also on the Russian River, for red sockeye salmon. They even brought their own equipment with them. That's pretty unusual. I usually provide the rod and bait for my clients, but people who are dedicated to catching fish like to do it on their own equipment so that they can go back and tell their friends that they caught it on their own rod and reel. I don't object to that. Whatever makes them more comfortable.

Some West German clients surprised me once. They caught a nice fish, about a forty-pounder, and wanted to have it mounted. That's no problem.

I called the mounter, Lynn Kennedy, down at Ninilchik Fish Mounts, and he came over. There was only one problem. They wanted to have just the head and tail mounted, instead of the whole fish. They wanted to eat the middle. That's all they mount on their walls. They want the head looking at you and the tail mounted with it. That's not the way I picture mounting a fish. That's how they do it in Germany, they said. You learn something new all the time.

It was a new experience for Lynn, too, and he'd been in the taxidermy business a number of years.

This German group fished on its own, too. They fished off the bank for Dolly Varden, and golly, they caught a seventeen-pound Dolly Varden, which is very unusual in the Kenai River. Most of the Dolly Varden I've seen weigh three or four pounds—some are even smaller than that. A seventeen-pound Dolly Varden is like a hundred-and-fifty-pound beagle.

So they caught a seventeen-pound Dolly Varden and took it to a place downtown for refrigeration so that they wouldn't have to carry it around until they went home. The day they were going to leave they went down to get it, and someone had stolen it out of the deep freeze.

They were mad, but they came back out to the river, went to almost the same spot, fished for an hour or so, and darned if they didn't catch another Dolly Varden approximately the same size. Two that big. Unbelievable. It must have been the twin brother of the fish that got stolen.

I've never really figured it out, but in my twenty years of guiding on the Kenai I think I've had people come fishing with me from about twenty different countries. I've had people from Sweden, Norway, Japan, France, Italy, Germany, Korea, England, Australia, Canada, Iceland—even someone from Nairobi, Kenya. He was a preacher. A church in town put him in touch with me.

I'm not sure whether or not I'm contributing to world peace, but I've had the West German chancellor out fishing, as well as the Japanese consul, fifteen reporters from Austria, West German television reporters, and outdoors writers from the top sports magazines in Japan. The top outdoors magazine in Japan sent over a reporter and did a story about me. The magazine compares to *Sports Afield* or *Field and Stream* in the United States.

I was getting so many clients from Japan over the years that I ended up printing brochures in Japanese. There's a picture of me and all the details about going fishing with Harry Gaines on the Kenai River. I send them to travel agents in Japan, and I've got a couple of friends who are Japan Air Lines pilots and live in Anchorage. They come out four, five, six times a year. And they always bring another group of Japanese with them.

My usual jokes just don't work because of the language barrier, but I find that foreign clients tend to entertain themselves. I use a lot of hand signals. Sometimes I feel that I'm the Marcel Marceau of the Kenai River. That's what it amounts to. You go slow. You show them what to do instead of telling them.

But I had these Japanese a couple of years ago who really buffaloed me. Things got off to kind of a strange start. They were here on business, visiting some of the fish processors. First of all, it was raining, and they all came over in business suits and dress shoes expecting to go fishing. I didn't have any rain gear for them, but I did have these fifty-five-gallon garbage bags.

So I cut holes for their heads to come through and holes for their arms to come through and they put them on. It was quite a sight— eight big, moving garbage bags walking down the path to the boat. They went on the river like that, four in my boat, four in another boat.

One of them got this big fish on. It was a monster fish, a really, really big fish. It was in the sixty-pound range. The fish began to run in circles skimming the top of the water. Right away I knew something was wrong because kings just don't do that. They don't surface. They stay down. I finally realized that the darned thing was snagged in the dorsal to come out of the water and do that. The hook was through the dorsal fin on the fish's back.

A snagged fish is next to impossible to land and bring into the boat. If you can't move his head, you can't control him. You have very little control with a snagged fish. It's also illegal to keep one. But I was letting him play it just for the fun of it. Normally, I'd cut the line right away and let it go.

They kept pointing to my net and I kept saying, "No, I can't net the fish. Illegal," I'd say. "Fish illegal. Cannot net fish." I kept telling them that over and over. They were still reeling it in and eventually got it close to the boat. They insisted that I get the net and bring in the fish. I said, "No, I can't do it. Illegal." The guy who had the fish on was backing up in the boat, and they were actually trying to reach down with their bare hands to grab it.

I kept saying, "Guys, you can't do that." I don't know how many times I told them it was illegal. There were people over on the bank watching what was going on, too. We were the best show around. Finally, the rod broke and the fish got away, and this Japanese who had tried before to tell me they couldn't speak enough English to know what I was talking about turned around, hit the bow with his hand, and said, "God damn!"

Perfect English. They'd been fishing with me for two years in a row, but they never came back after that. I think they probably got upset about the fish, but it was illegal to take it, and I wasn't about to break the law for them.

Or maybe they just didn't like their rain suits.

A Souvenir for the Wall

Sometimes I wonder what that guy in *Jaws* would have done if he'd actually caught that great white shark. It was a bit large to hang on the average living-room wall. Now the left-field wall at Fenway Park — the one they call the Green Monster — is just about the right size for a trophy like that.

There are misconceptions about what makes a trophy fish, or what makes a fish special enough to have it mounted, and size is part of it. The Alaska Department of Fish and Game considers any king salmon weighing seventy-five pounds or more to be a trophy fish. That's the definition for the record books. In my opinion, any salmon you catch can be a personal trophy. There's no strict rule about size. It can be a prize fish for anyone who catches it.

There's an image, perhaps perpetuated by the movies or television, that any fish that gets hung on the wall has to be just about the greatest fish ever caught — bigger than an eight-by-ten glossy photo, anyway. And that's just not so.

The majority of people who fish with us are one-time fishermen. They've either never fished before in their lives, or they fish very rarely. And, of course, most people who aren't from Alaska don't get the chance to chase big fish like king salmon. They've caught mostly small fish, so if they catch a twenty-five or thirty-five-pound king salmon it looks like a whale compared to what they catch back home.

People want to show that fish off. Sure, they can do it with a photograph. They can bring that fish in, take it out of the boat, hang it up, and pose with it while it's hanging on the scale. The fish looks awfully big dangling from the hook. There are several ways of

This is one hefty king salmon that did not get away from a Harry Gaines-guided boatload of fishermen. (Photo by Ken Graham)

showing off their prize and a photograph is enough of a souvenir for most people.

Or a fisherman can have that fish mounted. I have a taxidermist who's there every time my boat comes in, ready to take your order if you want to have that fish skin mounted. He's from International Taxidermy. They come up and spend the whole summer with me. They're from Washington State.

There are two different kinds of mounts. One is a skin mount. The taxidermist will actually skin the fish for you. He pulls out his knife, takes the skin off the fish, then he gives the fisherman the meat, which we package, and the client carries it home. Just puts it under his arm like a suitcase and carts it home on the plane in a nice carry-on bag.

The taxidermist takes the skin with him, and it's anywhere from six months to a year after that before you get your fish. The skin goes through a time-consuming process. It has to be soaked in certain salts, then it has to be stretched. Then it has to be put on a Styrofoam form, pulled tight. Then it has to be dried. All the oils have to come out of that skin. That's why it sometimes takes up to a year before it's done properly.

After that the fish is painted, artificial eyes are implanted, and it's made ready for shipping. So you can see that it's not a quick process, where the fisherman hangs around waiting as if he's just ordered a hamburger to go.

It's also a pretty expensive process. You really have to want to preserve that fish. The cost is around nine or ten dollars per inch, and the average size of a noteworthy king can be anywhere from forty-five inches to fifty-six or fifty-seven inches. So you're looking at $500, $600, or $700 to have a fish mounted with a skin mount.

We tell the clients one thing that happens with a skin mount is that it deteriorates over time. Nothing's forever, I guess. After ten or fifteen years that fish will begin to deteriorate and disintegrate unless you maintain it. You must paint them as often as you can. Then they may last a little bit longer.

There's also the fiberglass mount—the molded fish. This is a somewhat cheaper process. Bob and Ann James are masters of this method. They operate at Anchor Point, about an hour away.

We take the fish, measure the girth, measure the length, and make note of any characteristics—any distinguishing marks—that might be on the fish. We might even go so far as to take a photograph of it, if it's got some marks on it that aren't common. Like a tattoo that says Mom.

Just kidding.

Then we call Bob James and give him the vital statistics. We tell him exactly what your fish is like, and he'll make a mold that fits the description. He's done that so many times that he's got every size and type of fish that you might want. The molds are already sitting there. Maybe the dimensions will vary a half inch or so. Or if you want to take the fish over there, he'll make an exact mold of your own fish. Doing it that way will cost you about seven dollars an inch. It'll be $100 or $150 less than a skin mount, and you can usually get it within a week, unless it's the busy season. Bob James is a great taxidermist. He's stuffed and mounted bald eagles for the American Bald Eagle Foundation project in Haines, Alaska.

A lot of people who fish with me really want to mount a fish, but they do hesitate at first when they learn the cost. Then they find out that they won't actually get the fish back for six or eight months, and they can pay $50 or $100 a month until then, and they like the idea that they don't have to pay it all at one time. The installment plan — just like you're buying a major appliance. We may end up getting 150 or 200 fish a year mounted.

I have two fish mounted and on display on the wall in the living room of my home in Kenai. There's one king salmon and one silver salmon. I've caught a seventy-two pounder but mounted a forty-eight pounder. I've assisted in catching kings bigger than that, but a king salmon is a king salmon. They all look pretty big.

I caught my forty-eight-pounder in 1979, caught it in the river right in front of my fish camp. Quarter Mile Harry strikes again, right next to the property. Just living up to the nickname.

Someone who was there commented that it would make a beautiful mount. It was the way it looked, not how big it was, that made me take another look, and I decided, "Yeah, I'd like to have that one mounted."

I have never been out on the Kenai River seeking a big, big fish just to hang on my wall. I'm just always going after a king salmon every time I go out. I could have kept fishing and come up with a bigger one, but I decided then that it would be nice to have a king salmon on the wall.

It's not necessarily the size alone. I didn't really think about having a trophy for a long time, but eventually I thought I should have one.

It only makes sense. It's what I do. I catch fish. It's a symbol, I guess, of my career, of my twenty years on the river. It's not the biggest fish I've ever caught. Of course, I could take that fish Outside and show it to fishermen in the Lower Forty-Eight, and it would look like Godzilla to them. Just catching it was the real trophy for me.

The other fish I have mounted on my wall is a silver. It's twenty-one pounds. That's quite large for a silver, though I didn't think anything of it at first. There are two runs of silvers, both of them later in the summer, after the two king salmon runs are over and the king fishing season on the river ends on July 31. The fish in the first silver run will probably average nine to twelve pounds. The fish in the second run may go as high as fourteen, sixteen, or even seventeen pounds, average.

I was going to hit my silver on the head and eat it for dinner, but my wife, Dot, was there, and she said, "That's a big fish. You can't do that."

I said, "I'm going to eat it."

She said, "No, Harry, you've got to mount that fish. It's a twenty-one-pound silver and it's a beauty."

And it is a beautiful silver. It could win a fish beauty contest. No blemishes whatsoever. It's funny, during the season I'm either catching or helping people catch twenty, thirty, or forty silvers a day. Me mount 'em? I'd never even considered it.

But I finally did mount this one. Dot didn't help me catch it either. I caught it myself. If she'd caught it, I probably would have helped her lose it.

What people are really trying to do when mounting a fish—whether it's an official trophy fish or just one that's special to them for some reason—is to capture the moment—capture the experience—and keep it. They put that fish in their office or their home. I know of some people who have built a home around a fish. They'll design their fireplace and everything else to fit the fish.

I also know of people who aren't allowed to bring the fish they caught into the house. Take Dean Yeasel. His wife won't let him take his mounted king into the house at all. She doesn't care for fish, so he keeps it hung up in the garage. Dean has been fishing the river as long as I have—twenty years. He won the first Kenai River King Salmon Derby in 1971. He got a ribbon. I guess he can take that into the house.

Another reason that some men might go to the trouble of getting a fish mounted is to prove to their wives that they really went fishing. Did you hear the story about the fellow who left on a fishing trip, and when he got back home complained to his wife that he could never find his pajamas? "Well, that's odd," she said. "I packed them inside the tackle box."

Mounting a fish is just part of the experience, especially if you're not someone who fishes all the time. You get to take the evidence home and keep it. You don't have to brag about how big that fish was. You can just point to it and say, "I caught that big fella."

Wanted—Dead or Alive

The $50,000 fish has a nice ring to it, doesn't it? I thought so.

Back in 1979 I was sitting around one day, trying to figure out a way to increase business — how to get my share of the growing number of people who were coming to fish the Kenai River. What would set me apart? What could I offer to make those people fish with Harry Gaines? It was one thing to have a reputation — and I did. My name spread by word of mouth. But I wanted to attract customers from the people who'd never heard of me at all or who had never even been fishing. How could I do that?

Well, the idea I got was that I'd offer $50,000 to any person who caught a world record king salmon while fishing with me. I'd heard about some similar offer being made somewhere for something. I decided that that kind of promotion would have an irresistible appeal. That was real money then. Even in an era of million-dollar sports contracts, that's a lot of money even now for the average person.

At that time the world record was ninety-one or ninety-two pounds, and I felt that there were bigger kings to be caught out there. Can you imagine the publicity value of having the world's biggest king caught in your boat, with you as the guide? People would be lining up to go fishing with Harry Gaines.

And think of how many people would line up to try to catch that king salmon. That's where it would really pay off. There would be a great amount of publicity about me offering that big a reward. The news media would latch on to that. It had sex appeal. I was already imagining the kinds of newspaper headlines my offer would create. "Wanted — Dead or Alive." We could have made up wanted posters with a picture of a king salmon on it, just as if it were Billy the Kid or Jesse James. People would have wanted the posters themselves as souvenirs.

I got very excited about the idea. I thought I'd definitely hit on something that could really boost business and that would be fun in the bargain. If it's not fun, then it's not worth doing anyhow.

So I called up an insurance agent, Wayne Brown, at New York Life in Anchorage, and told him what I wanted to do. Who knows what the odds are on anyone catching a world record with me? But I did want protection in case it happened, since I don't have $50,000 lying around the house. I needed an insurance company to cover me with a policy for the reward money.

The agent in Anchorage contacted Lloyd's of London and laid it out for them. It must have sounded preposterous to them in London. A $50,000 fish? They bought the idea. They said they'd insure me. Do you know how much that insurance policy was going to cost me? Only $500. Heck, I would have gotten ten times the value of that in publicity just by making the offer.

I was all set to go.

But first I went to the Alaska Department of Fish and Game and told them what I had in mind. They regulate the river and supervise the fishing, and it just seemed like the right thing to do, as a courtesy. They don't generally like surprises.

I said, Here's what I'm fixin' to do, and I told them, and they went nuts. They went ballistic. They started pleading with me not to do it.

This was when there was tremendous growth on the river and we were just exploring ways to limit the number of guides and manage the fishing. They argued that it would generate too many people on the river, and it would become a circus, and blah, blah, blah.

My reply was that we were only talking about more people fishing with *me*. Fishermen weren't going to flock to other guides. They were going to come out with me because they could get the reward by catching the fish with Harry Gaines.

Well, their answer was that if I made the offer, other guides would make the same offer. Everyone would do it. I thought they might be right. At that time I still had a lot of faith in Fish and Game. I thought they were truly on the side of the sport fisherman. I've learned a lot since then, but at that time I believed in them and went along with their suggestion for the sake of the sport. So I canceled the whole plan.

Lo and behold, a few years later, in 1985, Les Anderson of Soldotna caught a world-record king on the Kenai River. His new record is 97¼ pounds. He wasn't even out with a guide. He was out with his brother-in-law, Bud Lofstad.

Actually, that's not even the biggest king ever caught. There was one that weighed about 130 pounds that was taken commercially in a fisherman's net about thirty years ago in southeast Alaska. That fish is on display at the Fish and Game office in Anchorage. Les's fish is on display at the Convention and Visitors' Bureau in Soldotna.

Les's new world record got me to thinking about the whole idea of the reward again. By that time I didn't really care if Fish and Game thought it was a good idea or not. *I* thought it was a good idea. I called the man at New York Life back. I told him to get me another quote for an insurance policy from Lloyd's of London. I wanted to make the $50,000 offer.

I was determined to do it. I believed my original instincts were correct and that it would have been great for my guiding business and would have sparked a lot of interest in fishing on the Kenai. Then the New York Life man called me back and told me that Lloyd's of London wouldn't touch it with a ten-foot pole. Lloyd's of London wouldn't do it? This is the company that will insure anything.

I decided that I didn't care whether I had the insurance or not—I was going to offer a reward for catching the world record king with Harry Gaines. But I'm not crazy, either, so the first reward I offered was $1,000. It didn't quite have the impact of a $50,000 reward: I think prize money that big would have made news around the world. The $1,000 reward got some attention, but it wasn't the same.

In 1988 I upped the reward to $5,000 and put it in all my advertising literature. "Come catch the world record with Harry Gaines."

That's a lot of money. It's not $50,000, but it's substantial, and maybe it's enough to make someone choose to fish with Harry Gaines rather than another guide.

No one's ever caught a world record with me, but that doesn't mean it's not going to happen. And the offer still stands.

Although you don't catch halibut in the Kenai River, there's a tremendous amount of halibut fishing in the ocean nearby. The town of Homer is a mecca for halibut fishing. People take charters out miles into the ocean for the whole day. And people can catch big halibut right off Anchor Point or Ninilchik, which is less than an hour from Kenai by car.

I heard one story about an elderly couple who caught a huge halibut off of Ninilchik that made me blink. Not everybody, it seems, cares about getting a world record.

Halibut are just unbelievably big. The expression we use to describe the three-hundred-pounders (and up) is Barn-Door Halibut. That's 'cause they're about as big as a barn door and just as flat. The world-record halibut is 450 pounds. Well, anyway, this older couple was fishing. They were in their late seventies or so. They were sitting in a fourteen-foot boat in the swells just offshore. They hooked into this very, very large halibut and somehow managed to overcome it and drag it into the boat.

They brought it in to the beach, got it out of the boat, and were in the process of cleaning and filleting this fish on the shore when a crowd started to gather. Other people saw how big it was and started telling them that it was so big maybe they shouldn't cut it up. By the time Fish and Game came down to take measurements, the fish had been chopped up quite a bit.

Do you know how big that fish was? Fish and Game estimated it was 470 pounds. It was probably a new world record. My God, if I had caught that fish, I'd have done it up in plastic.

To some extent, Les Anderson was the same way about his record fish. He just threw it in the bottom of the boat when he caught it and didn't rush back to the scales to weigh it. He kept on fishing and brought it in later. He didn't realize what he had. In fact, if he hadn't brought it over to his car dealership to show to his employees, he might never have weighed it. They were all over him to weigh it, so he did. Bingo. New record. But he didn't weigh it until something like six hours after he caught it.

That means it was bigger when he caught it — fish shrink over time. The blood, the juices run out. If someone out with me catches a big fish we get in to shore and weigh the fish on my scales at the fish camp as fast as we can. It may not be a record, but it might be an official trophy fish, and it should be recognized.

It's hard to estimate just how much weight is lost by leaving a fish lying around after it's caught. It's my experience that a twenty-five- or thirty-pound fish might lose a pound or so per hour for the first two to three hours. It doesn't sound like much, but how would you feel if you missed out on the world record by a pound—simply because you never got around to weighing the fish until it was too late?

It's never been one of my things to try to break world records. My goal is simply to go fishing, not to go someplace to try to set a record.

I'm a sitting-on-the-dock-of-the-bay fisherman. By that I mean I just like to fish a lot. I'll fish anywhere, in any weather, for any kind of fish. It must really be in my blood. I told you about my parents, but my sister Sarah and her husband, B. J., fish all the time, too. They live in New Mexico, but they travel all over the Southwest on fishing trips. Sometimes they come up to Alaska, but usually they'll spend a month at a time fishing lakes in Texas. And they're only out there catching crappies, tiny fish. Some people could come to Alaska and catch one fifty-pound king salmon and have enough fishing for a lifetime, but my sister and B. J. just love to fish. They'll fish for anything.

I have never been fishing outside of the United States or even in the state of Hawaii. I would like to go there to fish or to New Zealand and Australia because I hear that the fishing is great there. That's river fishing. I've talked to people who've been down there and they say there are salmon, as well as trout.

They do have some very large fish in the ocean there. Marlin and sailfish get up to several hundred pounds. I would get a thrill out of catching those. Maybe me going fishing for that kind of fish would be like the people from the Lower Forty-Eight who come to Alaska to go after the biggest fish they'll ever see.

Maybe I'll go off to that part of the world, down under, to go fishing when I retire. I'll retire from fishing to go fishing. What else would I do, when you think about it? I'm not about to retire from fishing to go to work in an office.

The biggest fish anyone ever caught with me was eighty-two pounds. It was in 1982. The man who caught the fish was Bill Brook, Sr., of Illinois.

He caught the fish about two miles north of the fish camp. What

I remember was that it wasn't very hard. It wasn't that difficult to bring it in, and it didn't take that long. Maybe ten minutes or less. Sometimes a larger fish is just like a heavyset person — and I pat my own bulging stomach when I say that. What I'm saying is that the maneuverability is just not there.

I have trouble putting on my shoes when I'm overweight. I wear out easily. Well, big fish do, too. If you get to reeling them in before they really know they're hooked, the first time they come up to the surface — and they will come up — you're going to get them into the net and into the boat.

If they ever sound — go to the bottom and sit there — it becomes a whole different battle to land them. The bigger ones in particular.

During the summer of 1989 we had a case where a man from Minnesota hooked a big fish. He hooked it and it stayed hooked, but the man couldn't bring it in. He and his guide — he was out with an inexperienced guide — let the fish sound, and the scene developed into something like *The Old Man and the Sea* — the tug of war of all time.

The fight with that fish went on for over thirty-seven hours. People were lining the bank watching the man in the boat and waiting to see the fish. Newspaper people were there and so were television cameras. It was said that this fish was a whopper, that it might be a new world record.

I was out there with my video camera myself trying to film the whole thing. Now I believe as much as anyone that there are big kings in the river and that there are kings that are bigger than the current world record. But I don't think this was a record fish. I saw it when it came up and rolled, and I just don't think it was that big at all. I think it was closer to a sixty-pound fish than the world record. That was a small fish compared to the record. I don't think it was even close to a record.

That fish went to the bottom and he stayed there. They were trying to nudge him back up using light-test line, twenty-five or thirty pounds, but with a large fish on you just can't horse him around. They let him rest. I wonder if that fish hadn't already spawned. It was deep red in color, which indicated it had been in the river for some time. Once fish have spawned they just find a place to sit and die.

Well, this fish kept going behind the rocks. The movement wasn't there. Usually, kings will fight and run, but he was just sitting there. He stayed in one place for something like sixteen hours. And when he did move, he didn't move more than twenty or thirty feet. He got himself right next to the bank and got comfortable. It never should have gone on so long. And then they lost him.

They took two nets out — because they didn't have one that was big enough — and tried to catch the fish with two nets. Whoever was driving the boat put it in neutral or something, and the boat drifted away from the fish so they couldn't reach out and get it when they got close. You've got to tire a fish out so that it doesn't have the strength to fight anymore. This fish was just taking a breather on the bottom, so when they got it up it could still fight, and when they tried to net it, it broke free and got clean away.

It was a great fish story, man against monster fish and all, but the fact is he should have got the fish, and I'm certain it wasn't a world record.

My strategy for reeling in a really big king, what we did when Bill Brook caught his eighty-two-pounder, is to reel it in quickly. The quicker the better. You reel fast and keep the boat even with him and net him as swiftly as he reaches the surface. That's with all kings, really, even the smaller ones, because, boy, if they get real active they'll just go all over the place. It's like roping a steer and trying to bring it down.

When Mr. Brook hooked that giant fish with me, we recognized right away that it was a big one. My first reaction was, "Damned big fish." I knew it wasn't a forty- or fifty-pounder, I'll tell you that.

Big king salmon generally are about four and a half to five feet long, fifty-five to sixty inches. Fifty-pounders measure out at fifty-four inches or so, and you'll find sixty- or seventy-pounders not over two or three inches longer. The girth is larger — they're fatter — the weight is around their middle. Like some people I know.

The average king is probably about forty pounds, and most of the kings that are caught are in the forty- to sixty-pound range. Fish that size are in both runs, in May and in July. The really big ones, bigger than that, just aren't there all the time. I don't know what the breakdown is, but I'd bet that only about 1 percent of the kings that are caught are in the eighty-pound range. Nobody keeps an eighty-pound king salmon a secret. They're more likely to rent billboard space. It's my guess that the biggest kings are only around for two or three days and then they're gone. They've moved on through.

I think the success rate for catching a king is about 60 percent for anglers who go with a guide.

Judging by my experience in my own fish camp, any time a sixty- or seventy-pounder is caught it is a rare happening. I have about six boats a day on the river most days during the king season, and up to ten or twelve on peak days, and I'd estimate that you're looking at only four or five fish a year that weigh over seventy pounds. If anybody tells you anything different, he's a typical fisherman — a liar.

I know there was one king taken in 1989 that was over ninety pounds. A young fellow from around here. The year before that there were two over ninety pounds.

As I said, every time I take someone out fishing I'm thinking we're going to catch the world-record king. That's the first thing on my mind. It's there waiting for us. And one of these days we're going to catch it.

I'll be happy to pay out my $5,000 reward when we do.

Fishin' and Talkin' Again

It's astounding how technology has shrunk the earth and how you can be fishing in the middle of the Alaskan wilderness and still be in touch with the outside world.

One time I had a big businessman, George Zamias, who is from a big city back east, out fishing. He builds shopping centers—big ones—all over the world. He was building a couple in Alaska and he came out fishing. He brought ten or twelve people with him, contractors he does business with, so we had quite a crowd.

We were out there for a little while when all of a sudden he said, "Damn." Then he said he had to go back to shore to make a phone call. The time difference—we're four hours behind the East Coast—meant that he had to do it right away. He didn't want to spoil the fishing, but would I mind taking him in?

I just smiled at him and said, "George, we're first class around here." I bent over, reached into the compartment under the steering wheel, pulled out the cellular phone I have on the boat, and said, "What's the number?"

When I was younger, radio was a big part of my life—for many years, bigger than fishing. And as fishing became a bigger part of my life, radio disappeared altogether for me—for a while.

But a few years ago I got to thinking and wondering if I could combine both of them. I called up a local radio station and said I thought it would be worthwhile to have fishing reports on the air, to let people know what's going on out on the river each day. You know, give them some guidance about where to fish, what is the best time to fish, and tell them whether or not the fish are biting.

That radio station could become known as the place to get the most up-to-date, reliable information, so it would help them. And, as you might guess, it wouldn't hurt me any to be identified as the guide who provided that information.

Originally I thought I might call in to the radio station, and they'd record a fishing report, and then they'd play it back two or three times a day. But we put our heads together and said that we'd do even better than that. We'd do the reports live. I was a little skeptical at first, since I knew how much equipment it would take to set this up. I said, "Well, that takes a radio and a transmitter," and they said, "No problem," so here we are.

My boat is wired for sound. I have a regular thirty-five-watt VHF transmitter that sends signals directly to the station. The first year we started — I think it was 1985 — we did it two or three times a day. It was great. We were the only ones doing it, and that made us the only ones with up-to-the-minute information. After all, I was out on the river all day. I knew what was happening. I knew when things changed, and most importantly, I knew if the fish were biting right then and there, not how they had been biting hours before, when a message might have been recorded. It was even better than my original idea.

The second year we upped the broadcasts to five or six times a day, and we now do up to ten a day during the height of the king season. We'd start out in the morning with the first report at 6:30, go every hour on the half-hour, take a break for lunch, and go through the afternoon and into the dinner hour. The last couple of reports I do from shore, when the boat is already parked for the night. That last broadcast isn't until 7:30 in the evening.

It's a lot of work, and you definitely have to watch the clock. If I get distracted, the station calls me, so it's not as if I can forget about an entire broadcast. The one agreement we have, though, is that if we have a fish on, I'm off the air in a flash. I can't be losing my clients' fish while I'm talking on the air. That would be very bad policy.

So if I'm in the middle of catching a fish, we might go on the air a few minutes late, or we might skip an hour. If someone gets a fish on when we start, I'll break off right in the middle of a sentence. I have to do that. It might be that fisherman's only chance at a king.

There's no set time limit for a broadcast and I'll sometimes banter back and forth with the disc jockey. He'll ask questions, or I'll tease him about his own fishing experiences. We could be on for two or three minutes. Some broadcasts don't last ten seconds if there's a fish on.

It's surprising how often that does happen. It can be the quietest fishing day in the history of mankind and then, bam! as soon as I go on the air, a fish will nibble at the bait. It happens very frequently. Maybe the fish pick up the radio waves and think I'll be too busy to bother with them if they steal the bait.

Once, we had just put out into the water near my fish camp. It was 6:30 in the morning and time for the broadcast. I had no sooner gone on the air with, "Hey, it's a beautiful day here on the Kenai," when wham! the rod goes down, bending in half, and I shout, "I've got to go! I'll be back!"

That time we got the fish — it was about forty or fifty pounds — landed pretty quick, and I called the station back and said, "I'm ready to go on. We'll go ahead and finish the report now." I put that guy on the air in nothing flat. It's great when you can put the fisherman on the air right away instead of waiting an hour because everyone's excited and full of energy. He's thrilled to death, hollering and shouting. I had one guy I was interviewing who had just caught a fish and I asked him what he thought about it and he said, "Aw, shit, that was fun!"

I blinked, I'll tell you that, but when something like that happens, I just try to keep my end of the conversation going. I kind of ignore what was said and hope no one will really notice and make a big thing about it. According to the Federal Communications Commission, if the use of an obscenity like that — a banned word — isn't planned, it's not a violation. It was in the heat of the moment. You hope that listeners aren't as focused as they might be if they were studying for the bar exam.

I had one guy on the boat from Atlanta, and his southern accent was a lot thicker than mine. I think mine's evened out over the years, what with all the time I spent in broadcasting and all the time I've spent in the North. But this guy really was from the Deep South. He made Jimmy Carter sound like he was from New York.

After this fella caught a king salmon, I put him on the air. I began by saying, "You caught yourself a king salmon."

He said, "Yes, I sho' did."

I said, "Well, what did you think about catching a fish that big?"

He said, "You know, suh, I've been to three country fairs, three hog callin's, and a pecker pullin' and I've never had so much fun as this."

I'm sitting there in the boat and I'm thinking, "A *pecker* pulling? What the hell is he talking about? And at the same time I'm pretty darned sure that I don't want him to be explaining that to me on the air. That was one time that I was caught by surprise. There were three or four seconds there when I was speechless. That very seldom happens. My wife Dot will tell you that.

I've had as many as three or four people in a day on the radio live. I just feel it spruces things up, adds an element of spontaneity to the fishing report. Sometimes I tell the people in advance that I'm going to put them on the air and sometimes I don't. A lot of times what they say on the spur of the moment has more meaning than if they've thought it through and rehearsed what they're going to say. I just poke that microphone in front of them and see what we get.

There may be some people who come out fishing with me on the Kenai River who think this is standard procedure—that if you catch a fish with anybody, the next thing you know you're on the air—but I think most of them know that I'm the only guide out on the river with live radio, and it's the only chance they'll get to talk about their fish like that.

The fishing reports have got me back on the radio year-round. I'm enjoying it all over again. In the winter I do a morning talk show, 6:00 A.M. to 8:30 A.M., with a couple of other guys. It's a three-man clown show is what it is, and we're liable to do anything on the air.

We do the news. We tell jokes. We read the horoscope. We talk about local people. One winter day when I was reading the news in a small studio, the other guys opened the door and put down a coffee can with plastic silverware and paper in it. Then they set it on fire. Just to keep me warm, no doubt. I'm in the middle of a sentence and start smelling smoke and seeing this fire and start laughing and choking. I'm trying to do the news and I can hardly talk.

The room was filling with smoke and small black particles were floating through the air. The studio filled with soot and I was covered with it. I guess I should have told the audience there was a report of a fire in the neighborhood.

That wasn't even the worst thing I had done to me on radio. Back in the 1950s, when I was working in Orlando, the guys actually

Live from the Kenai River, it's Harry Gaines! This is either a live fishing report for the radio, or I'm ordering a cheese pizza. (Photo by Lew Freedman)

undressed me down to bare nothing while I was on the air. In those days we used to do the news standing up. They came in and pulled off all my clothes. I finished that broadcast with my shorts down around my ankles. And I couldn't say a word while it was happening. I just had to keep reading the news like nothing was going on.

Returning to radio in Alaska led me into a new opportunity. A few years ago I got the chance to make some television shows about outdoor Alaska. I was the host, and each week I went out and filmed another adventure in the wild where I interviewed prominent outdoorsmen.

We used to have a TV station, Channel 17, down here on the Kenai Peninsula, and they liked to do some local programming. They came up with "Harry Gaines—Kenai Outdoors." It lasted for six months. I did twenty-six shows, and believe me, that was some pace.

We'd go out and film on Mondays, edit on Tuesdays and Wednesdays, and be on the air Thursday night. Some schedule, huh? It was a lot of work for a half-hour show.

About ten minutes of each show was an interview with someone from Fish and Game or a fisherman or an author who was an expert on the outdoors who had written a book. We had shows on fishing, clamming, hiking, backpacking—all different types of things you could do on the Kenai. We didn't get into hunting because we went off the air before the hunting season began. Probably just as well. You never can tell who would have gotten shot.

I went down to the beach in January when there was ice out there and dug up clams. We showed people how to go clamming. It was freezing. On the same show I might have a local author, Dan Sisson, come on and talk about the book he wrote about fishing the Kenai. Half the show was in the studio and half was on location.

Maybe my favorite show was the one I did with Les Anderson after he caught the world record. I just thought that was pretty special. Not many people can imagine a 97¼-pound king salmon. I mean that's the size of a person, and there is continuing fascination with that fish.

We went out on a boat with Les and Jim Repine, a man who was a well-known outdoorsman in our area. Jim had a television show in Anchorage for a number of years and wrote quite a few books about the outdoors. The three of us went out in a boat and we reenacted the catching of the world record. Of course, that fish wasn't available at the time so we had to use a substitute, but that's show business, right?

One thing I had to learn about television was the way it differed from radio. In radio you have to provide a lot of descriptive information because people can't see what you're talking about. Remember those baseball games we announced, where we provided the details of the play-by-play? On television, people can see everything, so your commentary has to have a different flavor. You don't want to repeat what they're already seeing — you want to add to what they're seeing. I had to get used to doing that. There's a tendency to talk too much. That might be the only time in my life when I found it was important to talk less than I was inclined to.

We even did a show where we cooked and baked fish on the air to show people what to do with them once they caught them. I can cook fish. After all the time I've spent around salmon, catching them and helping other people catch them, it would be ironic if I didn't eat fish, but I do. You might think I'd be tired of eating salmon, but I just never get enough of it. It's one of my favorite foods.

There are several ways I like to cook salmon. The first way is to roll it in corn meal and flour and then deep fry it. A second way is to bake the salmon using mayonnaise, onions, green bell peppers, lemon, and barbecue sauce for flavoring. You wrap it in aluminum foil and bake it over charcoal anywhere from thirty minutes to an hour on a side depending on how large the fish is. And you can also cook salmon soaked in teriyaki sauce.

In fact, with all the fish we've brought in over the years, there was an incentive to find ways to make them taste different. You've got to have those different recipes.

Well, that was one thing that got me to thinking that maybe the fish have different tastes, too. Maybe they get tired of plain old salmon eggs every time. So I concocted my own fish sauce, "Harry Gaines's Fish Scent. It's not a sauce for people, though there was some suspicion around here for a while about what went into it, since I also owned a restaurant.

This is not a sauce that you put on fish when you cook them. It's a sauce that you use on your bait when you put it in the water to attract fish. The main ingredient is something we've used for a long time to attract fish. I can't tell you what it is. I can't give away my secrets. Some big company could come along and steal the formula and make its own fish sauce.

It's a liquid sauce that comes in plastic bottles and it's red, red, red. Dark red. You squirt it on your bait, or you can take a cotton ball, put that on the hook, and spray the sauce on it. You're creating artificial bait, and when the sauce disperses into the water, it attracts fish.

Fish have a very sensitive smelling organ. It's been shown scientifically that they can smell as little as one part per million of a substance. That's how sensitive that organ is. So if you're upstream, and there's a fish downstream, and you want it to come to you, squirt a little sauce on your bait.

The sauce comes in two-ounce bottles. They sell in the store for $3.99. The sauce is for fish who have good taste. Any type of fish, not just salmon. It's an attractant, just like perfume on a woman is for a man.

And it works. I'll give you an example: at the fishing show they have every year in Anchorage they have a little trout pond. The little kids go and fish for trout. They are supposed to be able to catch fish easily. The idea is not only to provide them with some entertainment, but also to get them interested in the sport. The theory is that if they fish at this little indoor pond they might like to try it for real and go out fishing with Dad. It also keeps them occupied while Dad goes around shopping at the booths.

Except this one time the kids were fishing and the fish weren't coming to the bait. That's not a good situation—to have kids standing around with their fishing poles not catching anything. It gets discouraging and that's exactly the opposite of the point of the whole thing.

I had a booth at the show, and the people running the show came over and got a bottle of sauce, then went back to the pond and poured it in. The fish just ran for it. It was amazing. You had to be there. After that, I couldn't keep it stocked. It was an unsolicited testimonial right there and everybody saw it happen. Everyone came running over to buy the product.

Selling fish sauce might be my next part-time job since the TV program is long gone. It was kind of a hectic schedule anyway. The hardest part was trying to keep up with the production schedule once the fishing season started. I was out filming on Sundays and particularly on Mondays, when the Kenai River is closed during the king season.

It was a real challenge and I had a lot of fun with it. But the TV station folded. I guess our ratings weren't high enough. We probably weren't even a blip on the Nielsen charts. And there just wasn't enough advertising money around on the Kenai Peninsula to support the show—or the station.

But I'd like to think everybody was too busy fishing to watch TV.

Silver Is as Good as Gold

To fish for silver salmon in Alaska, you've got to be the hardy type. If cold weather bothers you, forget it. Of course, if cold weather bothers you, you shouldn't be in Alaska in the first place.

The silver season on the Kenai River begins August first and runs through October. By then we've usually had our first snow of the season in southcentral Alaska, so if you're the type of fisherman who wants to laze around and get a tan while he's fishing, you're definitely in the wrong place. By the end of the silver season you've got to be bundled up in long underwear, have something pretty thick on your feet, and be wearing a good, solid parka. Before we pack it in for the year, those little holes on the fishing rod where the line runs through will be frozen from the spray. The line's passing through icicles.

As you might imagine, fewer of the people who go silver fishing are in Alaska on vacation at that time of year. It's past the peak of the tourist season. But the silver traffic is heavy. You can have forty, fifty, or even a hundred boats on the river on a good day at the height of the season.

We are building a clientele of sportsmen who come to Alaska just for the chance to fish for this type of fish. The interest in silvers has grown, at least partially by word of mouth from people who've come to Alaska to fish for kings first. They get interested in trying something else.

September is the best time for silvers. That's when the second run starts, and none of the fish have been caught in drift nets because the commercial fishing season is over.

Chris Batin is a noted author of fishing books and magazine

articles who lives in Fairbanks. He came silver fishing with me many years ago just to see if you can catch silvers from the back of a boat with salmon eggs. I showed him that you can and he wrote about it. He was really fascinated by it. At that time most people fished for silvers by casting, using artificial lures. He put my method in one of his books and it got some attention.

King salmon get more publicity, and I suppose they deserve it, because there's nothing like them. It's awesome to take those huge fish. But fishing for silvers can be more fun because they're a more aggressive fish. They're more active and they bite more often.

When a silver takes the bait of salmon eggs, it gets quite active. One time not long ago we hooked into a fifteen-pounder and it went there and there and there, around and around the boat, before we finally got it in.

Once a silver is hooked, everyone else quickly reels in and stays in their seats. The fisherman stands up and follows the fish around, reeling all the time. You can't jerk the rod, especially before the hook is set, but once you're sure the bait's been taken you've got to keep the line tight. If you're reeling at the same time, it doesn't take long to get that fish.

The fish will squirm and try to run, sometimes even behind the boat and then back to the other side, and you've got to keep the rod high and not get the line caught on the console, but if you're reeling properly, the fish isn't going to go anywhere.

In some ways, fishing for silvers is more fun than fishing for kings. There can be more action. They're easier to catch because they're more plentiful, too. So instead of a limit of one king, a fisherman can catch three silvers per day. And when the silvers are biting good, we limit out. Once you get your three, you've got to put your pole down. Can't be greedy.

Don Peterson, a retired United Air Lines pilot from Salt Lake City, comes to Alaska to fish for silvers with me. He is one of the few fishermen I know who prefers fishing for silvers over kings. There aren't many who do.

Talking about Don reminds me of another fisherman from Utah, Dr. Max Blackman, a dentist from Provo. Dr. Blackman is a man with a great sense of humor. He sent me a necklace that he made out of king salmon teeth. Kings do have teeth. They measure an inch or an inch and a half long. It's a very crude necklace. It's definitely not for formal occasions.

More recently, he sent me a photograph of a mounted king salmon. Only this king had antlers. His letter informed me that this unique, one-of-a-kind fish (which resembled a jackelope if you ask me) was caught right in front of the Harry Gaines fish camp. The only one ever taken, he said.

You bet.

Kings, of course, are much bigger fish, but silvers are still quite a bit bigger than almost any other kind of fish caught in other parts of the continental United States. The biggest one I've ever seen I caught myself: a twenty-one-pounder. We've had plenty of eighteen- and nineteen-pounders caught, but even a six-, seven-, or eight-pounder is a very nice fish. An eight-pounder caught by someone fishing with me during the 1990 season measured twenty-five inches long, with a thirteen-inch girth, for an example. The catching of that fish is something you'll hear about a little later on. The silver is a large fish in its own right.

Silvers also have slightly different behavior than kings, and over the years you get to recognize their habits and target spots in the river where you're most likely to find them.

Kings go to the deepest channels, but silver salmon hug the shore, and where the bank sticks out they have to swerve out farther. The edge of a point of ground is a good place to set your anchor. Silvers will almost always be on the shallow side of the river. They do cross over sometimes, because of tides or the wakes of boats, but not in great numbers. Many of the best fishing spots are right over gravel bars. The silvers will be close in to the bank and also in shallower water.

August and September in Alaska look and feel like late autumn in the rest of the country. The leaves on the trees are turning yellow, but the sun isn't as hot, and it's more likely to be cool and overcast. This is the rainy season in southcentral Alaska. In 1989, it rained just about every day for six weeks straight. It was miserable.

When it gets rainy, the water on the Kenai River gets muddy, and that hurts the fishing. A fisherman can never see below the surface on the Kenai anyway, but if the water is murky the fish will go right past the bait without seeing it. If you think of fish in terms of shopping, then grabbing the bait is an impulse buy, just something that fish sees on the shelf and thinks he's got to have. If he doesn't see it, he won't be attracted, and it won't cross his mind that he must have red salmon eggs. Although you might think so, since that's how people are, the eggs don't really represent a treat between meals for the fish. They're just being aggressive.

Since he can't see beneath the water anyway, an inexperienced fisherman might get overly enthusiastic thinking he has a bite when his pole begins to bend and pull, even though he's just snagged on the bottom or some drifting piece of wood or brush. We call the thick pieces of grass people hook on to Kenai River salad. And I've seen many a twig or small branch that had a fisherman excited about his catch. I always tell those people that's where Mrs. Paul gets her fish sticks.

The fall, our fall, I guess you could call it, is a strange time. It's strange to be sitting in a boat fishing for silvers and see dead pink salmon floating past. Sometimes they're right on the surface, and sometimes they wash up on the bank. The wakes of the boats wash them toward the shore and they get caught in the rocks. Then the sea gulls eat them. It's a free meal for them. Fish the gulls miss might get lifted back into the water when the tide comes in again and buries the shoreline. Then they float on out to sea.

These are pinks that have already spawned. They don't eat again, and they slowly die. Occasionally, they're still twitching. You might see one that has its head just above water trying to get air. It will be dead soon. You may see twenty or more of them in an afternoon of fishing.

It seems like a waste for them to just die like that, but then they do become food for other fish. It's all part of nature's grand plan.

The moose-hunting season starts September first, and the Kenai Peninsula, with its thick foliage, is home to a lot of moose and bears. Hunters can find themselves in the same predicament fishermen more often find themselves in during the summer — competing with a bear for food. The bear is usually going to be the winner in that kind of confrontation.

Strangely, in all my years on the Kenai River, I've seen bears only three times.

Now most people who don't live in an area where bears are common don't have the proper respect for them. They've seen them in zoos, or they've seen them on National Geographic specials and think they're all cute and cuddly. Some have even seen them in the wild, from the bus in Denali National Park, and they get the idea that they can walk up to a bear and feed it or that bears won't bother them. Those people just aren't thinking with all the brains the Lord gave them.

There are a lot of myths about bears. Some people say that bears are scared of man and will always run the other way if they encounter a human. Some people say bears will attack only if you get between a sow and her cubs. But the truth of it is that there is no rule, there is no true law that you can follow and be sure. The only thing you do know is that the bear is bigger and more powerful than you are.

One time I had a bear cub come right into my fishing camp — which consists of a few trailers, a Porta-John, and some bunkhouses — climb up a tree and stay there. Now that's something that makes you nervous. You've got to think that Momma bear is close by somewhere — and not in the best frame of mind, wondering where Junior went.

Well, this little black bear cub scampers up a tree and stays there. I don't know if it was scared or what exactly, but it made itself comfortable on a tree limb and wouldn't budge. It stayed up there all day. We watched it and waited for the mother to come along, but she never did. The cub eventually left sometime during the night. It was kind of cute, but I wasn't sorry to see it go.

Only once did I actually see a bear on the Kenai River. That time was a few years back. I was in my boat headed down river a couple of miles from my camp and I came around a bend. There was a bear in the river, swimming away from shore. It seemed to be headed across the river. Oh, I'd say it was a quarter of the way across. But when it saw me or heard the motor on the boat, it turned around, swam back to shore, hustled up the bank, and disappeared into the trees. It just ran away. That's the best kind of bear confrontation for a man — when the bear is more frightened than the human.

The one time I did have a true bear encounter, about five years ago, I wasn't even fishing. I was out moose hunting with a friend and we were trudging through deep alders, pushing them aside. You couldn't see more than a few feet in front of your face.

We were pushing our way through this brush when we came to a clearing. And there was a black bear standing there about fifty feet away. There was nowhere to run, even if I'd wanted to, since that is not the method you're supposed to take with bears as they can cover ground much faster than you can. The bear could have covered that ground in seconds. Bears can move faster and more explosively than any Olympic sprinter. Anyway, the alders were too thick to run anywhere without quickly getting tangled up.

I was thinking, "Where will I go?" There were no trees to climb, either, and you can never be sure that will work.

Well, the bear stared at me and I just froze. I couldn't even talk. My friend came up and said, "I see it." I raised my rifle and pointed it at the bear, but I didn't shoot. I just stood there aiming at it and being scared.

It's illegal to shoot bears in Alaska unless it's in defense of life or property or unless you have a permit for a legal hunt. I didn't want to shoot the bear. I didn't want this to become a case of "in defense of life." It was my life here. I just wanted the bear to go away.

The bear stood up on its hind legs and stared at me. Then it snorted, threw its head back, and ran away.

It made me think that it was a lot safer catching fish than hunting moose. I've never had a silver salmon maul me.

One of the best places to catch silvers on the Kenai River is Eagle Rock, about twelve miles from the mouth of the river. It's no secret. Some people go out at four o'clock in the morning to get a good spot along the shore there, and the boats line up in both directions as far as you can see. It's as crowded as New York Harbor on the Fourth of July when the tall ships are there—the boats anchor about ten yards apart.

There's no telling just what path the fish will take. Sometimes you can be precisely in a spot that was good the morning before, but this time the fish will swim right past you and the boat behind you will catch them all. They'll get several fish and you'll get none. There's not a thing you can do about it. It reminds you that fishing is not as scientific as chemistry.

I have noticed this: When I mention on the radio that one place had good fishing between ten and eleven in the morning, the next day between ten and eleven in the morning there will be a crowd of boats out there.

Eagle Rock can also be one of the coldest places on the river to hunker down. Being on the river is always colder than being on land. There's nothing to shield the wind, no trees to break it. And it's particularly cold when you're moving. You're creating your own windchill factor. You've got to wear a hood and you'll want to turn up your collar so that your neck doesn't turn numb from the cold.

The problem is that you've got to be prepared to sit in a place like Eagle Rock for hours at a time. Sometimes the wind calms down and it's absolutely still. Then it can be beautiful sitting there. There is often an eagle in a tree just in from the shore. We had an eagle family living there not too long ago, with a big thick nest. The daddy eagle would perch on a tree about thirty yards away and keep an eye on it.

Periodically, that eagle would fly out above the river, wings spread, just soaring, then dive bomb into the water, just like a plane. He'd scoop up a salmon with his talons — he never lost his catch — and fly back to the nest with it to feed the babies. Sometimes, he'd fly across the river and come back with a stick in his talons. Just a little fix-it job for the nest. I wasn't sure why he was still working on the nest in early September. It seemed it was time for the babies to leave and go out on their own.

When it's sunny and there aren't many clouds, you can see Mount Redoubt clearly in the distance. That's the volcano that erupted in December 1989, just before Christmas. It grounded all the jets for a few days and spoiled a lot of people's Christmas vacations. It kept erupting once in a while for months after that and coated the peninsula with ash. We had dirty snow, so when you walked on it the grime stuck to you, and it crunched in a different way than frozen snow ever did. It made a mess on the streets, too, and the ash was so thick that it turned the whole sky dark. People who went outside were walking or driving around wearing those white surgical masks to keep from breathing it.

From my winter home in Kenai, which is about fifteen miles or so from my fish camp, you look right across the water at the mountain. It's beautiful on clear days — a very special view, like having your own personal mountain in the backyard. But it was both fascinating and a little unnerving during the period of the eruptions. The power unleashed was something to see.

One winter morning when I was getting up early to do a radio show, an eruption started, spewing ash and steam. It was thundering and lightning and it looked like the end of the world. I was only half dressed and I ran out there in my long johns with the video camera and got it all on tape. I also covered some of the eruptions for Cable News Network.

Sitting in a boat on a sunny day looking at the snow covering the peak, though, you'd never guess it could be that violent. It looks like a painting against the blue sky. On days like that you think about how nice it is just to be outdoors in Alaska. But on days when the sky is completely gray and it's raining on you, or if the wind is whipping in from shore across the tall grass, you're reminded that winter is coming and the fishing season will be over soon.

A lot of people ask me if an old fisherman like me who spends so much of his time on the river, fishing in the spring, summer, and into the fall, ever goes ice fishing. Well, I've been ice fishing just three times and I found it to be too cold. It was too uncomfortable sitting out there. Ice fishing is a surefire way to freeze your rear end off. I may get cold fishing for silvers, but at least I'm not going to get frostbite.

I did go ice fishing and caught lake trout. Good sized ones, too. But there was a problem there as well. They were covered with parasites. It kind of turns you off to see that, although when you bring a fish in and lay it on the snow the parasites die pretty quickly and just fall off.

Another drawback to ice fishing is that you need the right equipment to drill the holes through ice that is three or four feet deep on a lake. What I like to tell people is that I used to go ice fishing, but when it took us almost eight hours to chop a hole big enough for the boat, I was too exhausted to fish, and I just gave it up.

The Summer of 1990

The summer of 1990 was probably the weirdest summer of fishing I've ever experienced in my two decades on the Kenai River.

There were no fish.

Well, that wasn't exactly true, but there weren't as many fish as we've had in past years and there weren't as many fish as we were counting on. The case of the disappearing fish. We needed Perry Mason on that one.

There were shortages of king salmon, reds, pinks, silvers, all of the fish that are on a three- to five-year spawning cycle. As a result, the Alaska Department of Fish and Game stepped in with all sorts of restrictions and put several kinds of limits on the sport fishery.

The first run of kings enters the Kenai strong in the late spring and runs into June. The second run of kings comes into the river around the first of July. But Fish and Game sonars showed the fish were not returning at the rate they had set in order to preserve the fishery. As I have said before, you can set your watch by the arrival of the kings, they're that reliable, but not so in 1990.

We had already been under restrictions limiting the type of bait we could use, and then Fish and Game was forced to restrict us to catch and release at the end of the first run, rather than shutting down the river outright. But it had practically the same effect. At the end of the second run (in July) they went to catch and release again. There was fear of not getting the proper escapement, the proper number of fish coming through to keep future runs alive.

The catch and release rule is horrible for the sport fisherman, the type of client we guide, and for most of the people who come to Alaska and to the Kenai River to fish. Catch and release means you can still fish the river, but once you hook a fish you have to let it go. You have to release it. That does take some of the fun out of fishing. Most of the people I know want to take their fish home. About 100,000 people a year fish the Kenai River and when they catch a fish they want to keep it. You can't blame them. A lot of them have spent a lot of money for the chance to get one.

There are a lot of true sport fishermen who have their hearts set on catching a king salmon. They love to fish, and our business has been directed to the client who wants to catch a fish, keep a fish, and put it in his freezer. That fisherman pays $100 to $125 for a half day of fishing with a guide (not to mention the cost of getting to the fishing site) and he is not excited by catch and release. He does his fishing for two reasons—to catch a big fish and to keep a big fish.

This was the first time I experienced a season like 1990. We've had slow years, either because of water conditions or because of other natural, non-man-made conditions, but there's never been anything to compare with that year's lack of fish.

I'm honest in my business. I call people and let them know exactly what the conditions are and let them make the decision. There's a loss when I do that because some people make the choice not to come and fish with me, but I feel there's a gain, too, because you're being truthful with people. They appreciate that and they remember that. I hope that when they are again ready to fish they'll remember me and say, "Well, that guy Harry Gaines was straight with me. I want to give him my business."

We had a lot of cancellations. As soon as Fish and Game invoked the catch and release rule I called people all over the United States to tell them. About 70 percent of the fifteen hundred people a year who fish with me come from outside of Alaska. A lot of them decided not to come to Alaska at all. They put off their fishing trips for another year or until who knows when.

You know, the Kenai River gets a lot of publicity. The 1990 problems were reported in the *Wall Street Journal,* in *USA Today,* and on CNN. You know how people read things and misinterpret them. They thought the whole fishing season had been canceled. People were continually calling and asking if the river was really closed for the year. Well, the river wasn't closed, but it was a panic of sorts.

Now this is the way I prefer to do my weight lifting. Enough reps with a king salmon will build strong muscles. (Photo by Ken Graham)

And it's detrimental to the future. People plan their trips and vacations and they think, "Well, they shut down the Kenai River last year. The fishing isn't so good up there anymore," and they make other plans. This is a business I've spent twenty years building and I hope it doesn't take five or six years to rebuild.

Of course, we really don't know what will happen in the future. The summer of 1990 could very well have been an aberration. That seems likely. There've never been two slow years in a row.

What did happen? Where did all the fish go? You can't go back four years and say that something happened to disrupt the fish. There's no evidence of that. My only theory was that our fish were intercepted on the high seas. I believe the catches by foreign fleets, the incidental catches of fish that they aren't even interested in keeping, is the most serious problem facing Alaskan sport fishing.

The Japanese, the Taiwanese, and the commercial fishing fleets of other nations put out those huge drift nets and just scoop up tremendous numbers of fish. They've got nets that are miles long. They may be fishing for herring or another species of fish, but they catch everything. They haul up the salmon that are headed for Alaska and the Kenai River. From what I read about the sophisticated equipment and fishing procedures of the Japanese, the Taiwanese, and the Koreans, they've got it down to a science.

This is a very tough situation because we don't really know where the salmon go or where they come from when they return to Alaska to spawn. People keep saying there is no proof that the fish are being intercepted because no one sees it happen, and no one knows if those fish were headed for Cook Inlet or Bristol Bay. But it would be pretty coincidental for all those different kinds of salmon to come in lower numbers for no known reason. Further research may show that there was something in the ocean that killed the fish, but the foreign fleets are the most obvious reason. Those huge trawlers pick up everything on the ocean floor like vacuum cleaners. It's such a waste. They kill everything, including dolphins, seals, and other sea life. All the resources, all the fish, are being affected by it.

High seas fishing is a political issue. Our government could control it overnight with a trade embargo, though. The United States government must put pressure on the governments of other countries. Different methods must be explored.

The commercial fishing industry is also big business in Alaska, of course, and those nets pick up their share of the incidental catch. They do it in Alaska waters and they can have an impact. Their prime fish was the red sockeye and they picked up 200,000 silvers as part of their incidental catch between July first and August fifteenth. That's why the second run of silvers in September is so much stronger. They're not affected by the commercial fishery because it doesn't operate at that time. They also take a lot of king salmon headed for the Kenai River.

The Alaska commercial fishery is affected by foreign fleets, too. It's not just the sport fishery. If the catch is taken on the high seas, it can't be taken offshore of Alaska. Stands to reason.

Yet to those of us who make our living through sport fishing it sometimes seems that Fish and Game favors commercial fishermen. I'll give you an example. Commercial fishermen are allowed to have a test period for their equipment, and in 1990 they caught a couple of thousand kings during that time. Even if foreign fleets were depleting them, a couple of thousand kings made the difference between shutting down to catch and release and staying open for the usual king catching period. Sometimes I wonder if Fish and Game remembers that sport fishing is a seventy-seven million dollar industry in southcentral Alaska. Their own figures say that sport fishermen spend thirty-eight million dollars a year in Kenai alone.

Some people still did go out and fish for kings during the catch and release period. Just to have the experience, I guess. Or they were here in Alaska already, and it was too late to change their vacation plans. But I'll tell you, just about the hardest thing of all when fishing for kings with someone you know is going to release that fish if they get one is the idea that you might hook into the world record.

There's a tremendous mystique about the world record and I've had that $5,000 reward going for awhile now. Wouldn't it be something if someone caught the world record king and had to release it? We did have a ninety-five-pounder caught early in the summer, a fish close to that 97¼-pound record, so the big ones were out there. Can you imagine having to throw back a hundred-pound king?

There was a lot of talk when the regulations were first imposed about just what you would do if that happened. The fine for catching a king and keeping it during that period was one hundred dollars. Lots of people said it would be worth it to pay the fine and keep the fish.

I thought about that some myself. There's a temptation. I jokingly said if we got a world record I'd find some way to put it on my ticket. I said I'd pay the fine. But then I realized I couldn't jeopardize myself by doing that. A client couldn't deal with throwing that kind of a fish back in the river and I couldn't either, but the state would probably do more than fine me if I did keep a fish like that. They'd probably take my permit away. Fish and Game would probably say something like, "You know better than to do something like that." There is more at stake than the fine.

Picture that. Catch and release and you catch the world-record king salmon. That really would have been the all-time story about the big one that got away.

Top Ten Fishing Tips
from Harry Gaines

There are right ways and wrong ways to fish, just as there's a right way and a wrong way to do anything else.

Now the right way to go fishing is to go with Harry Gaines.

I'm only kidding . . . that's a good way, not the only way. But there are important things to know if you're going fishing. Fish don't magically jump onto your hook, and if you go to the wrong place or don't know what you're doing, then many birthdays may pass you by before you even see a fish.

These tips are for catching salmon on the Kenai River, but many of the principles apply to fishing anywhere in the world. Here's hoping that these suggestions point you in the right direction — where the fish are.

1) Keep Your Bait in the Water
Now this may seem obvious, even to a person who's never been fishing in his life, but the basics are important. Clearly, you're not going to catch fish if you don't have your hook in the water. That's really fundamental.

You can waste a lot of time running up and down the river, looking for the right spot. All the time you're moving you have the hook up, out of the water, and that is all wasted fishing time. Keep the bait in the water as much of the time you're out on the river as possible. For sure the fish is not going to jump into the boat or your lap to grab the hook, and the fish is not going to jump onshore to grab the hook. I've never yet met a fish that had that kind of curiosity.

If you're fishing on a river for salmon, you're fishing for migrating fish. So they're constantly coming. Why move all over the river? If you spend more time and effort in a given spot, the odds improve that you're going to catch fish.

Now then, fishing in lakes is a little bit different. There are no obvious channels the fish travel along so you have to come up with a pattern, a strategy, to find out where the fish are. That's either the depth they move in or the location they gather in. You've got two things to worry about and figure out.

One way to locate fish in lakes is to know the temperature of the water. Up here in Alaska the water temperature is always pretty cold. There aren't many lakes that people will swim in, even on the Fourth of July, because the human body prefers water that is warmer than sixty degrees.

What you need for lake fishing is a way to measure the temperature of the water. Look for water that's usually between thirty-five and forty-five degrees. If you find water that cold you're going to find fish. You definitely aren't going to find swimmers out splashing around and interfering with your line. Unless they need rescuing, that is.

If you haven't got the gadgets you need to measure the temperature, you're going to have to look for the fish. So you set a pattern, just like a grid. You'll go from north to south or east to west, and you'll move over thirty feet maybe, again and again, until sooner or later you find the fish. It's almost as if you're mapping the lake.

In the Kenai, in river fishing, it doesn't work that way. If you get the right spot, if you know the channels, the fish are going to come to you.

2) Get the Proper Equipment

You can't get anywhere without the proper equipment. You can't fish for king salmon with dynamite. Although it might work, it's against the law.

You need the proper rod for king salmon, a medium or heavyweight rod. This will depend on your own skill and expertise and the experience you have. If you're a novice you might want to go with a little heavier type of fishing rod, until you're accustomed to fighting and working the fish and bringing the fish in. Unless, of course, you've got a guide with you who can give you information about what to do.

Normally, a guide will work you through, talk you through, bringing the fish into the boat, and you'll be using light to medium gear.

If you're fishing from the bank, you've got to take into consideration the area you're in. If you've got a large fish on, do you have enough area to move around to bring that fish in? You can't be bumping into trees or tripping over boulders. You've got to watch what you're doing or you can hurt yourself. When your focus is on the fish it's real easy to lose track of where you're going. Next thing you know, boom! you've hit your head on a low tree branch, the rod is pulled out of your hands, and not only does the fish escape, but there's your rod floating downstream, too. Tsk, tsk.

Do you have the proper tackle? Don't fish with light tackle from the bank unless you have a lot of area to move around. Again, it depends on your expertise. Having a boat standing by in case you do hook into a large fish is always a good idea as backup if you're fishing from the bank. Be prepared for all eventualities.

Bait-casting reels are what you want to use on large fish. That's because there's going to be a time when you're going to have to play that fish, and the line will be going in and out, straight in and out, on a bait-casting reel. On a spinning reel, every time you twist the crank you twist the line, and so you're continually turning that line, twisting it, and it weakens the line. Sooner or later the line will birdnest and you've got a real mess. A lot of people use a spinning reel, but I'm telling you the best thing to use is a bait-casting reel. The line goes straight in and out, and there are no weak points.

Keep the fish as close to you as possible. Keep working that fish and keep him as close as you can, because the farther away the fish gets, the more advantage he has. The fish will either break the line or come out of the water and spit the hook. In a place like the Kenai, a fish can hide on the other side of a rock or a downed tree and you'll never get him out.

One other reason that it's important to keep the fish as close to the boat as possible, at least here, is the crowding on the rivers. So many people are out fishing — and some of these Alaska rivers are so accessible — that with all that traffic, if the fish gets too far away from the boat someone's invariably going to run over your line and snap it in half. It just happens. Or maybe the fish will get up underneath somebody else's boat and you've got a problem getting it back out. You'll probably lose the fish. You've got to keep him close to your boat so you can gradually reel him in and net him.

And don't let that line touch the boat in any way. If the fish makes a dart, if it makes a move to go to the other side, you've got to work it around the bow to the other side. If you don't, the fish will just break the line every time.

Another essential piece of equipment is a net, if you're fishing for king salmon, and make sure you have the right size net, too. When Les Anderson caught his world record king down here a few years ago he didn't have the right size net. They tried to net the fish four or five times. He had a borrowed net that day and it had a small hoop. He just couldn't net the fish. They finally beached it on a gravel bar after an hour or so. He was lucky it didn't get away. Can you imagine that, losing a world record?

When you go fishing for king salmon on the Kenai River you don't know what's on the other end of that line. When you get a fish on, you don't know whether it's a hundred pounds or if it's a twenty-five pounder. So you've got to carry the right equipment with you at all times.

You wouldn't go hunting for bears with a pop gun, would you? Same thing.

3) Use the Proper Bait

Most guys will tell you what they're hitting on, what the fish are biting on. They'll probably let you know what they're using. Or, if you have to, just educate yourself with your eyes. Watch what people who are catching fish are using and bring that next time.

Check colors. Colors are very important. There is a wide variety of artificial lures. The standard colors are silver, blue, and a combination of those. Those are real popular. And greens, reds, blues and greens, and chrome will also do the job. Of course, much of the time we use salmon roe, the little red salmon eggs.

The way the law reads, you've got to use artificial lures up until about the ninth or fifteenth of June, and then we go to bait. The changeover comes after the first nine thousand fish have entered the river. Subtract those that are caught and you have the escapement.

The Fish and Game officials have specific numbers they watch for to ensure the future of the fishery.

The Alaska Department of Fish and Game thinks it's a little harder to catch fish with artificial lures. My personal theory is that if everybody is using almost identical lures up and down the river, the fish may just decide they're part of the scenery and bypass them. It becomes hard to catch fish at all. I think the best thing to do is to switch to other lures from time to time.

4) Be Aware of the Weather

This is certainly an important aspect of fishing in Alaska. It's usually ten or fifteen degrees cooler on the river than it is on land.

The wind makes it cool out there. Don't be fooled if it's a sunny day. The sun may seem hot, but if you're moving up and down the river, you're creating wind, and it's cold. Bring a jacket or a sweater and expect it to feel like autumn, even if it's not.

Then, of course, it rains quite a bit on the Kenai Peninsula, so you have to be prepared for that. A fisherman who is too optimistic will pay for it. Remember, Alaska is different from anything else you're used to.

I've seen people who are underdressed get borderline hypothermic while on the river. It's real easy to do so, especially if the sky clouds over and you get wet when the temperature is forty-five degrees. It's a misconception that it has to be extremely cold for you to get hypothermic. It happens even when it's only cool. When the sky is blue and clear on the Kenai it's really God's country, just the most beautiful place on earth. But when it turns rainy the sky turns the color of slate and just hangs there, and you can get a mean cold moving in just like that, as fast as you can snap your fingers.

You always want to be sure to bring rain gear. Stay warm. Wear long underwear and an extra sweater. It's always better to overdress and take pieces off if you're too warm than not to have the pieces of clothing to put on.

I used to tell people from California — and I made a mistake — to dress for their fall time of the year. Well, fall time of the year to them is maybe wearing a long-sleeved shirt. So they would come out fishing without even a sweatshirt for a top layer. They were always freezing.

So I don't do that any more. It's a different type of cold up here.

5) Don't Fish Alone

The Kenai River is a beautiful river, as pretty as a postcard. When it's that glacial green it looks like the kind of ocean water you see in the Caribbean. Kind of pale and light. But just because it's pretty to look at doesn't mean it can't be dangerous.

The water's moving fast. There you are in a boat by yourself and you hook a king salmon, a big, powerful fish. First of all, you're trying to bring it in yourself and keep an eye on which way your boat is turning in the current. That's already too much to worry about by yourself. Then if you reel the fish in, you're trying to net it by yourself. I have seen people do it, but it is not easy. It's just not a one-man show. You need somebody with you for safety. Take a kid when you go fishing, to steady the boat and to assist. It's that extra pair of eyes that helps you and lets you concentrate on bringing in the fish.

Every year you hear stories about people drowning in Alaskan waters while they're out fishing. It happens all the time. This is a very rugged place and people have to respect it. The weather changes abruptly. The water can change abruptly. You've got to be smart, and one of the most important things to be smart about is recognizing what you can and cannot do.

6) Use the Proper Boat

The Kenai is a fast-moving river. There are wakes created by other boats. You get knocked around quite a bit. Boats less than fourteen-feet long, with less than a twenty-inch gunwale, are just not the thing. You need a nice, durable boat on the river.

The last drowning we had on the river was in the late 1980s. The people fishing were in a twelve-foot boat with about a fourteen- or sixteen-inch freeboard. A man got thrown out of the boat. He was flipped over the side. He crossed over somebody's wake and the choppy water just threw him right out. It happened at Eagle Rock at eleven o'clock at night.

Make sure you have the proper-sized boat, one that will offer you protection.

7) Be Safety Conscious

Setting out in the proper boat is only the start. There are many other things to remember to bring with you so that you'll definitely come back to land.

My fishing tips should help you satisfy even the heartiest appetite.
(Photo by Ken Graham)

Be sure to have life jackets. You do not want to be out on the Kenai River, or any body of water, without a life jacket. Wear that life jacket.

Be sure you have a fire extinguisher. You need a sounding device, such as a whistle or a horn, to alert others if you get into trouble. I have a whistle tied to the console of my boat where I can reach it while I'm steering. You're required to have some kind of noisemaker that will attract help. Standing up and yelling and waving your arms might not get the job done.

Be sure you have an anchor. You need to throw an anchor out if your engine quits so you can come to a stop if you can't get to the bank. There are sweepers all over the river. Sweepers are trees leaning into the water. If you go underneath one of those with just the speed of the water, without power, you can end up capsized. Maybe your boat's going to be full of water. Or maybe the sweeper will throw you out and you'll injure yourself.

Something that the average person might not think of — that he should — is being sure he knows the river or the area he's fishing in very well. And going to the same place from one year to the next isn't all it takes to be knowledgeable.

These rivers have massive gravel bars and they change from year to year. The ice moves things around. There are new channels, and old channels are blocked off because of shifting gravel. So just be sure you know what's going on.

8) Bring a Good Attitude

Be a good neighbor on the river. Don't go out with the idea that you're the only one out there, and everybody else should get out of the way. There's a lot of people on the river and you've got to respect their space.

The river is big, the river is wide, but it isn't always big enough for everyone who wants to fish for salmon on the same day. Take your turn drifting. Go all the way up to the end of the hole and then drift back all the way through it. Don't head in on somebody.

You have to be polite. There's no reason for people to be snarling and yelling at each other while they're out on the river. You're supposed to be out there to have a good time. You can't have a good time if you're yelling and screaming. You'll end up with heartburn.

Part of the good attitude you need to bring when you go fishing involves how you think.

I know your idea is that you're going to catch fish or you wouldn't be there. But you can't expect it. The fish might not be biting that day. You might come in right at the end of the king run. There's no God-given right to catch fish. You can't be sitting in the boat all angry if you don't catch one. Your attitude has to be, "Hey, if I catch one, I'm lucky." You are lucky if you catch one. Only a small percentage of people catch fish in any given hour on any given day.

You have to be determined to go catch fish, but you can't let it ruin your day if you don't. You can't let it destroy you. There's always next time.

9) Know the Law

When I first started guiding on the Kenai River more than twenty years ago, it was wide open. There weren't any guides and there weren't many fishermen. That also meant there weren't many rules or regulations, because they weren't as necessary as they are today.

Everything's changed now. There are so many people fishing the Kenai that it would be like one of those rasslin' free-for-alls — where they all gather in one ring and the last one standing is the winner — if there weren't any rules.

You have to know your regulations these days, or you can get in trouble with the Alaska Department of Fish and Game.

First, make sure you have a license. A resident license costs ten dollars. An out-of-state person's license is ten dollars for three days. It changes, though, so don't assume. The state is going to take its bite before you can find out if the fish are biting, but it's not that expensive.

Recently, the state added a new item — harvest tickets. You've got to have them on your person and you've got to punch them right away. You've got to cut out the month and the day. "Immediately upon catching and retaining a king from Cook Inlet or Kenai Peninsula waters, you must validate the ticket." That's what is required. You've got to keep the ticket with you in case you get stopped by a Fish and Game officer. You get the harvest tickets free when you buy a license.

There are many regulations. Your guide will know them, but if you're going out by yourself there are several things to be aware of.

Know the bag limits. You can catch only one king on any given day on the Kenai River, and you're allowed only two for the season now. But you are allowed to catch up to three more kings in other areas of Alaska during the season. You cannot bring a fish out of the water if you're not going to keep it. If you catch a king salmon, and you decide you want to release it — if you don't think it's big enough would be one reason — you can do that. You can't bring the fish out of the water, though. If you do, it counts against your bag limit. You've got to remove the hook or cut the line.

One of the major regulations on the Kenai River is the limit on boat engines. They can't be more powerful than thirty-five horse-power. It affected a lot of people when they put that in.

Treble hooks can't be over half an inch from shank to point. That was never enforced until recently. It means that some manufactured hooks can't be used anymore. Some hooks are a little bit larger than that. They're about five-sixteenths of an inch. We had to change all the hooks on our manufactured lures for one-sixteenth of an inch.

10) Go Fishing with Harry Gaines

I'd love to have you.

Seriously, why should you come fish with Harry Gaines? I can't give you a guarantee that you will catch a fish. No guide can do that.

We do absolutely guarantee one thing, though. If you go fishing with Harry Gaines, you are guaranteed to have a good time. I'd take an oath and swear to that.

Postscript—
A Miracle Has Occurred:
Lew Freedman Caught a Fish

I had made four attempts over four years to nail myself a king salmon. And not even the generous, knowledgeable assistance of fishing guide Harry Gaines made the slightest impact on the fish. For four years, I'd been shut out.

Clearly, this called for a total revision of strategy. Rather than go through another long Alaskan winter mumbling about my bad luck and lamenting my still-empty freezer, I changed tactics.

I went fishing for silvers.

Desperate measures for desperate situations. Perhaps, I reasoned, the sophisticated Freedman-detecting sonar perfected by the kings hadn't been passed on across species lines. Maybe the silvers weren't as intelligent. Maybe the silvers weren't as technologically wise. Maybe they hadn't heard of me.

Now over the years I had developed a following of sorts for my fishing trips. Friends came up to me with advice. Strangers called with advice. I was going at the wrong time, to the wrong place, in the wrong weather. There was also a body of opinion that I would never, ever catch a salmon unless it rained for forty days and forty nights and a couple of fish swam over to my house seeking refuge.

Harry Gaines, my trusty fishing guide, was trying to overcome all the damage I was doing to his reputation. A couple more trips out with Harry without me catching fish and he would be taking early retirement.

The first time I went silver fishing the waters of the Kenai turned brown so fast you'd have thought we were out there making chocolate pudding and spilled some—like fifty tons of it. The fish couldn't have seen our bright red salmon eggs with a flashlight, so we knocked off.

I wasn't going to let that fishing season pass without catching a fish, though. It's one thing to miss out on kings, but silvers are more abundant, more user-friendly, and should be much easier to catch.

So I went back a second time. Harry, Dot Gaines, and I had been out for a few hours, and things were tame and didn't look promising either. Then Dot landed a silver, showing it could be done.

It was just before 5:30 in the afternoon, and Gaines had the microphone for his regular fishing report nestled in the palm of his hand. It was showtime. I said, "Uhm, Harry, I think there's something happening here." I don't know if I've ever seen a more surprised man in my life.

I had always wondered if I'd be able to tell when I got a bite. I figured I'd miss it completely, just think I'd snared some piece of debris on the river bottom. But you can tell. It's a good, solid tug when a fish bites, and the rod starts to bend in half.

Gaines's face lighted up as if he'd just realized he'd won a million dollars in the lottery. He started shouting into the mike. "We've got a fish on here. I've got to go. The fish have been kind of scarce, and we're going to take this one."

We were.

The fish took the bait and pulled. I stood up in the boat and reeled. The fish ran, looping around the back of the boat. I raised the rod high over the console and reeled. The fish swam back to the side of the boat. I moved back to the side of the boat and reeled. The line was coming in, and so was the fish.

Within a minute the fish broke the surface, wiggling and flopping and trying to free itself. I reeled and brought it to the side of the boat, and Gaines leaned over with a wide-mouthed net and swooped it up as if he were scooping ice cream. He lifted it over the side of the boat, bashed it on the head a few times, and tossed it into a metal tub.

A fish! Unbelievable. It had silver sides, blood where the hook had sunk in, and it was just lying there flat. Dead.

Harry considered it a vindication of sorts. If Lew Freedman could catch a fish with Harry Gaines then anyone could.

"Finally!" he yelled. "Congratulations!" He got down on his knees in the boat and faced me. "Congratulations. Congratulations."

Did this excited reaction mean that perchance Mr. Gaines had wondered if I would ever catch a fish? At least in his lifetime?

"I had my doubts," he said. "But it did happen. At 5:30 P.M., September 5, 1990, Lew Freedman caught a fish. Unfortunately, we'll have to have a little funeral ceremony because that was my trained fish. He was supposed to tease you, but he took it a little bit too far.

"Put the line back in," added Gaines. "You're hot."

Hot? Right. That's like someone breaking out of a one for twenty-five batting slump with an infield single being told he's hot.

But I wasn't hot. That was my only fish. My only fish? That was enough. Gaines picked up the fishing rod and whispered into the reel, "Thank you. Thank you very much."

You think he was relieved? You think I was relieved?

We motored back to the fish camp, weighed and measured the fish. It was this big—eight pounds, twenty-five inches long, with a girth of thirteen inches. (Remember the fish Harry was talking about during the silver season?)

It really is hard to believe that the world's worst fisherman finally caught a fish after all these years. It was probably the world's dumbest fish.

Do you think there's a king salmon out there in the Kenai River with the same low IQ?

—Lewis Freedman

Lewis Freedman is the sports editor of the *Anchorage Daily News* in Anchorage, Alaska. He has won numerous state, regional, and national journalism awards and is also the author of *Dangerous Steps: Vernon Tejas and the Solo Winter Ascent of Mount McKinley.*

Other Stackpole books by and about Alaskans

Dangerous Steps: *Vernon Tejas and the Solo Winter Ascent of Mount McKinley,* by Lewis Freedman. "A great twentieth-century mountaineering adventure, and a superb fireside read (with down booties and hot chocolate)." *(Booklist)* Paperback, $14.95, Canada $19.95.

The Last Great Race: *The Iditarod,* by Tim Jones. "One of the most knowledgeable Iditarod writers around, Jones . . . captures the character and culture of the various checkpoints along the way. With a reporter's eye for detail, he conveys the stark splendor of the country and the competition without falling into lyrical excess . . ." *(Associated Press)* Paperback, $14.95, Canada $19.95.

Race Across Alaska: *First Woman to Win the Iditarod Tells Her Story,* by Libby Riddles and Tim Jones. "This fast-paced description of [Riddles's] bout against both the elements and veteran competitors generates electrical excitement." *(Publishers Weekly)* Paperback, $14.95, Canada $19.95.

Shadows on the Tundra: *Alaskan Tales of Predator, Prey, and Man,* by Tom Walker. ". . . an understated and beautifully written memoir of twenty-odd years in the arctic backcountry." *(Gray's Sporting Journal)* Hardcover, $19.95, Canada $26.95.

With Byrd at the Bottom of the World: *The South Pole Expedition of 1928–1930,* by Norman D. Vaughan with Cecil B. Murphey. ". . . a fascinating glimpse at the life of a man driven by nonconformity and the thirst for adventure, as well as an enlightening look at a too often forgotten yet honorable moment in American history." *(West Coast Review of Books)* Hardcover, $19.95, Canada $26.95.

To order books, call 1-800-READ-NOW, toll free.